THE HOLY LAND IN COLOUR

by Sami Awwad

PRINTED IN THE HOLY LAND

Distribution:

Jerusalem
Sami Awwad
The Mount Scopus Hotel
P.O.B. 19702
Jerusalem
Phone: 284891-283746

The United States of America
Lewis Rukab
2986 Oak Isle Road N.
Jacksonville
Florida 32217
Phone 904-2681466

Canada
Mrs. Kathryn C. Purvis
R.R. 7
Pembroke Ontario
Canada K8A 6W8

Australia,
New Zealand, The Pacific Islands
Lawson Partners Pty. Ltd.
37 Kendall Street West Pymble
Sydney 2073 N.S.W.
Australia
Telephone 498-4984

Republic of South Africa
Baptist Publishing House
P.O. Box 50
Roodepoort 1725
R S A

England
Willard Thompson Ltd
Grafton Place
Worthing
West Sussex BN11 10X
Phone 0903 209983/4

PRODUCED BY PALPHOT LTD.

THE HOLY LAND

The Holy Land is located at the extreme eastern end of the Mediterranean. It is bounded on the north by Lebanon, on the east by Syria and Jordan and on the south by the Sinai desert. The Holy Land is small in size (about 14,000 sq. miles), but it has played a great role in human history. In ancient times it was crossed by the most important lines of communication which linked up Egypt with Syria and Mesopotamia. In modern times, it has always been a land of unrest because of its being the land of the three great monotheistic faiths, and part of the Middle East, which is the bridge between three continents. This is the land where lie the ruins of the world's most ancient civilizations, the land which throughout its long history was the meeting place between East and West, the land of the prophets and of Christ, who, with their immortal teachings and laws, directed the course of humanity towards justice and law by producing the three monotheistic faiths, Judaism, Christianity and Islam. To the Jews, this is the land of the Bible and their past glories; to the Christians this is the land where Jesus lived and suffered, the land which heard His mighty words and witnessed His miracles; to the Moslems this is the land where the prophet ascended to heaven. From the most ancient times until today came pilgrims from every land enduring fatigue and discomfort, braving all kinds of perils, to see this land of great history and faiths, this land which had been familiar to them since their childhood. This land of faith and love, has also been a land of war, blood and misery. Since very ancient times until today, war followed war, riot followed riot, saturating its holy ground with human blood. No country in the world has had a more dramatic history than the Holy Land. Here, in brief, are the main historical outlines of the Holy Land.

Archaeologists tell us that the Holy Land was occupied as early as 9,000 B.C. by the oldest known communities on earth, but its written history began with Abraham when he arrived in Canaan from Ur in Mesopotamia in approximately 1950 B.C.

1250 B.C. Joshua crossed the river Jordan, conquered the land of Canaan, and divided it amongst the twelve tribes.

1200 B.C. The Philistines from Crete invaded the land, and the land of Canaan was called after their name "Palestine."

1025 Saul was crowned the first King of Israel.

1004—965 David reigned as King of Israel.

965—922 Solomon reigned and the Temple was built and dedicated.

953—930 Israel was divided into Israel and Judah.

721 the Assyrians captured Samaria and took the ten tribes of the Northern Kingdom into captivity, thus ending the Kingdom of Israel.

587 Nebuchadnezzar destroyed Jerusalem and the Temple and took the tribe of Judah into captivity in Babylon.

539 Cyrus conquered Babylon and allowed the Jews to return to Jerusalem. The Temple was rebuilt by Zerubabel.

334 Alexander the Great conquered Palestine and after his death it was controlled by the Ptolemies of Egypt.

198 Antiochus III of Syria defeated the Egyptians and Palestine passed into the hands of the Seleucids.

175 Antiochus IV became King. He abolished the worship of Jehovah and desecrated the Temple by offering swine on the Temple altar.

167 The Jews, led by an aged priest Mattathias and his sons, revolted against the Seleucids and defeated them.

64 B.C. Pompey conquered Palestine.

40 B.C. The Parthians surprised the Romans and captured the land.

39 B.C. Herod the Great expelled the Parthians and reigned until 4 B.C.

4–1 B.C. Jesus was born.

30 A.D. Jesus was crucified.

66 A.D. The Jews revolted under the Zealots.

70 A.D. Titus crushed the Jewish revolt and completely destroyed Jerusalem.

132–135 The Jews revolted a second time under the leadership of Bar Kokhba. The revolt was crushed by Hadrian who destroyed Jerusalem and rebuilt it as a Roman city called Aelia Capitolina.

330–634 Palestine passed under Byzantine rule. After Constantine's conversion, Christianity spread rapidly. Many churches were built.

614 The Persians invaded Palestine. Thousands of Christians were slain and hundreds of churches were destroyed.

636 The Moslems conquered Palestine and made Jerusalem their third sacred city.

1009 Fatimid Khalif Hakem destroyed the church of the Holy Sepulchre together with many other Christian buildings sparking off the war and animosity for 200 years between East and West in the great collision of the Crusades.

1099 Jerusalem was captured by the Crusaders and the Latin Kingdom was established in Jerusalem.

1187 Saladin, a Moslem prince from Egypt, defeated the Crusaders at the Horns of Hittin ending their Kingdom of Jerusalem.

1263 the Mameluke Sultan Bibars of Egypt captured the remaining Crusader strongholds and the Mamelukes held the coastal cities for the next 250 years.

1400 Mongol tribes under Tamerlane invaded Palestine.

1517 The Turkish Ottoman Empire conquered Palestine and held it for 400 years.

1917 Palestine was taken by the Allies in World War I under General Allenby. This was the year of the Balfour Declaration for a Jewish National Home in Palestine.

1922 The British Mandate over Palestine was confirmed by the League of Nations.

1947 The United Nations adopted a plan of partition of Palestine between Israel and Jordan.

1948 The British Mandate ended and on May 14th the Jewish National Council established the State of Israel. War began between the Jews and the Arabs.

1948 War ended and an armistice was signed between Israel, Egypt, Syria, Jordan and Lebanon. Palestine was partitioned between Israel and Jordan.

1967 June 5. War broke out between the Arabs and Israel. It ended after six days of fighting with Israel occupying the entire Sinai peninsula, the Golan Heights and the West Bank of the river Jordan.

1973 October 6. Another war broke out between the Arabs and the Israelis. After sixteen days of fighting a cease fire was reached. We hope and pray that peace will come in the near future; that both Jews and Arabs who lived peacefully together for centuries may find peace after decades of animosity and that both will work together again for the prosperity and the future of this land.

Aerial view of Jerusalem

Jerusalem, standing high amidst the poor Judean hills, has been crowned as queen of the world's cities for 30 centuries. Blessed with nothing material, it was chosen by God to be the bulwark of monotheism. From its barren hills, the philosophers, the prophets and Christ launched the eternal laws of moral and brotherly love. From its ground spread the flames of faiths which established the rule of justice and religious beliefs between people blinded by error and idolatry. "For out of Zion shall go forth the Law and the word of the Lord from Jerusalem." It is the religious capital of half of the human race. To the Jews it is the symbol of their past glories and the hope of their future. To the Christians it is the city of Jesus' last ministry, the city which saw Jesus die and arise from the dead. To the Moslems it is the city where the Prophet Mohamed is believed to have ascended to heaven. Jerusalem, source of faiths and peace, the world's most sacred city, has been also a city of terror, war and blood. The sword has been devouring its children throughout its long history. There have been more wars fought at its gates than in any other city in the world. To walk in and around Jerusalem is to walk over a sea of human blood. Jerusalem has been besieged more than 50 times, conquered 36 times and destroyed 10 times.

The origins of Jerusalem are lost in the mists of antiquity. It was first mentioned in the Bible during the time of Abraham under the name of Salem which means peace; "And Melchizedek, King of Salem brought forth bread and wine, and he was the priest of the most High God." (Gen. 13:18)

In the 10th century B.C. David captured the city from the Jebusites, made it his capital, and brought into it the Ark of the Convenant.

965—922 B.C. Solomon beautified the city and built the Temple.

587 The Babylonians captured the city, destroyed the Temple, and carried the Jews into captivity to Babylon.

538 The Jews returned to Jerusalem and rebuilt the Temple.

332 Alexander the Great captured Jerusalem.

168 Antiochus Epiphanes razed its walls.

167—163 The Jews enjoyed independence under the Hasmonean Kings.

63 The Romans captured the city.

37 B.C. Herod was appointed King of the Jews. As a great builder, he beautified Jerusalem, built its walls and rebuilt the Temple more magnificently than Solomon's. Herod's Jerusalem was the city that Jesus knew.

70 A.D. In fulfillment of the prophecy of Jesus (Luke 19:41—44, 21, 20—24) Jerusalem was destroyed by Titus after the crushing of the first Jewish revolt.

132—135 After the crushing of the second Jewish revolt of Bar Kokhba, Hadrian rebuilt Jerusalem as a Roman city and called it Aelia Capitolina. Roman temples were built over Jewish and Christian sacred sites. The Jews were forbidden to enter the city under penalty of death.

330 Constantine converted Jerusalem into a Christian city.

614 The Persians conquered Jerusalem and destroyed all its churches.

636 Jerusalem passed to the Arabs who held it for almost 500 years.

1099 Jerusalem was taken by the Crusaders and became the seat of their Latin Kingdom.

1187 It was reconquered by the Moslems under Saladin.

1517 The city fell into the hands of the Turks and remained under their control for the next 400 years.

1917 It was taken by the Allies under General Allenby of the British Army.

1948 During the Jewish-Arab war, Jerusalem was partitioned between Israel and Jordan.

1949 Jerusalem was made the capital of the State of Israel.

1967 During the Six Day War, Israel took the Old City, which had been in Jordanian hands, and Jerusalem became united once again.

Dung Gate

St. Stephen's Gate

Damascus Gate

THE WALLS OF JERUSALEM

"Our feet are standing within thy gates, O Jerusalem, Jerusalem that art built as a city that is compact together".
Psalms 122:2:3

The present impressive walls of Jerusalem are additions from different periods of construction. They were rebuilt in their final form as they appear today by the Turks, under their great ruler Suleiman the Magnificent in 1542 A.D. In these walls, which are $2\frac{1}{2}$ miles in circumference and average 40 feet in height, there are 34 towers and 8 gates — the New Gate, Damascus Gate and Herod's Gate in the northern wall; St. Stephen's Gate and the Golden Gate (closed by the Turks in 1530) in the eastern wall; the Dung Gate and the Zion Gate in the southern wall and the Jaffa Gate in the western wall.

Zion Gate

The Golden Gate

Herod's Gate

THE CHURCH OF ST. ANNE

When the Crusaders were driven out of Jerusalem, they left behind them more than 30 churches built during their time. St. Anne's Church which is the best preserved, is one of the finest examples of their construction. It was built in 1100 A.D. by the wife of Baldwin I in the Romanesque style. It is built over a crypt venerated as the birthplace of Mary and the home of her parents Joachim and Anne. After the defeat of the Crusaders, Saladin turned the church into a school of Islamic theology. In 1856, following the Crimean War, Sultan Abdul Majid gave the site to Napoleon III as a reward for his help during the war. The church was restored and given to the White Fathers.

THE POOL OF BETHESDA

lies a few yards from St. Stephen's Gate inside the walls of Jerusalem. At the time of Christ it was just outside the northern wall of the city. It stood near the Sheep Gate which led into the Temple. It was a meeting place for invalids as its water was believed to have healing properties. The pool is sacred to Christians since here Christ healed the man who had been crippled for 38 years (John, 5). The pool, buried under debris for hundreds of years, was recently in great part unearthed by the White Fathers. It was found that the pool was rectangular in shape "about 350 feet long by 200 feet wide by 25 feet deep" surrounded on all four sides by porches and divided laterally by a 5th porch. This confirms the words of St. John who described the pool as having 5 porticos. One of these pools was used for the washing of sheep brought to the Temple for sacrifice. Remains of an enormous 5th century basilica, built by the Byzantines and destroyed in 614 by the Persians, were discovered. The Crusaders built a chapel over the ruins of the Byzantine church. The facade and the main entrance of this chapel are still visible above the remains of the pool.

Antonia Tower Model

THE ANTONIA FORTRESS

When Herod the Great rebuilt the second Temple, he rebuilt and enlarged the castle which stood at the northwestern corner of the Temple. He named it Antonia in honour of his friend Mark Antony. It was built in the form of a massive square with four strong towers. According to Josephus, the inner part was the size of a palace with all the necessary conveniences. The western third of the Antonia was covered by an impressive paved square, "Lithostratos" in Greek, which was used by the Roman legionaries for training, parades and games. The Antonia was the last scene of the life of Jesus. Very early on Good Friday morning, Jesus, having been condemned by the Sanhedrin, was led from the house of Caiphas to the praetorium at the Antonia. Within the precincts of the Antonia, Jesus was mocked, scourged, crowned with thorns and condemned to death. The Antonia, razed to the ground by Titus in 70 A.D., covered with debris and buildings for centuries, was uncovered little by little. The site is occupied at present by a Moslem school, a Franciscan convent and the convent of the Sisters of Zion. The courtyard of the school is held to be the site where the private part of Jesus' trial took place (1st station of the cross). In the compound of the Franciscan convent there are two chapels, the chapel of the Flagellation, marking the traditional site where Jesus was scourged and the chapel of the Condemnation, marking the site where Jesus was condemned to death. The convent of the Sisters of Zion contains the most impressive remains.

The Lithostratos

CONVENT OF THE SISTERS OF ZION

"He (Pilate) brought Jesus out and sat down on the judgment seat at a place called The Pavement".

John 19:13

This convent was founded by a French converted Jew, Father Alphonse Ratisbone from Strasbourg. Father Ratisbone came to Jerusalem in 1855 and bought the land beside the ancient arch of the Ecce Homo (Behold the Man). The ruins were removed and in 1859—64 he built the convent of the Sisters of Zion. In 1931—37 Mother Godeleine and Father Vincent of the Ecole Biblique of Jerusalem excavated the site. The pavement about which St. John wrote 20 centuries ago was discovered; "He brought Jesus forth and sat down in the Judgement seat in a place that is called the pavement." (John 19:13) This pavement, named Lithostrotos in Greek, was the scene of the public trial of Jesus. Here Pontius Pilate moved his tribunal to be near the rioting crowd waiting outside the Antonia Gate. Here he presented Jesus scourged and said, "Behold the man" and here he finally washed his hands and condemned Jesus to death on the cross. This pavement, which was at the ground level of the city in Christ's time, is the actual courtyard of the Antonia where Jesus was condemned to death and where he started the way of sorrows, the way of the Cross.
to death and where he started the way of sorrows, the way of the Cross.
The paving stones trodden by the feet of Jesus are striated in a manner to prevent horses from slipping, and, there are channels in the pavement to collect rainwater into the large cisterns beneath, capable of holding millions of gallons of water.

THE KING'S GAME

Traces of games played by the Roman soldiers are carved on the surface of some of the stones. One of the games played with dice, the King's game, could have been used with Jesus as its subject (Matthew 27:27–30, Mark 15:16–20). They used to choose a burlesque king, mock him and then put him to death. The pavement is one of the most interesting sites in the Holy Land.

"Shuk" oriental market scene

"So they took Jesus, and he went out, bearing his own cross".
John 19:17

THE VIA DOLOROSA
(Way of Sorrows)

is the traditional pathway Jesus followed carrying the cross from Pontius Pilate's judgement hall where he was condemned to death, to Calvary where he was crucified. The events of this sorrowful way are commemorated by 14 stations of which nine are related in the Gospel and five in tradition. The first two are located within the site of the Antonia, seven are located in the streets and the last five are located within the church of the Holy Sepulchre. Each Friday at 3.00 p.m. a ceremony, led by the Franciscan Fathers, is conducted along the Via Dolorosa.

THE ARCH OF THE ECCE HOMO

named after the words of Pontius Pilate "Behold the man" has no connection with the events of the passion of Christ. It is part of a Roman triple gate leading to Roman Jerusalem, built by Hadrian in 135 A.D. Part of this arch is incorporated in the church of the Sisters of Zion. Tradition relates that it is built over the site where Pontius said "Behold the man." Another tradition states that the stone on which Pontius Pilate stood when he said "Behold the man" was incorporated in this arch.

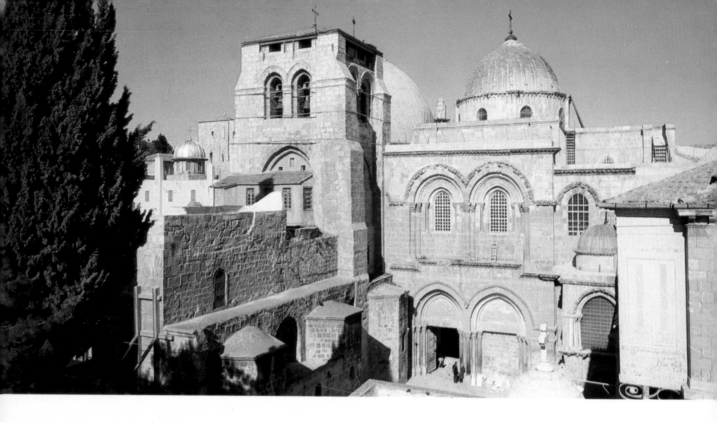

CHURCH OF THE HOLY SEPULCHRE

"So they took Jesus and he went out, bearing his own cross to the place called the place of a Skull, which is called in Hebrew Golgotha (John 19:17)." The church of the Holy Sepulchre, which is the most sacred place of Christianity, stands over Golgotha, the place of the Crucifixion and the tomb where the body of Jesus was laid. The Crucifixion took place outside the city wall "Which was without the walls but close to the city." (John 19:20). Since its first construction in 324, the church of the Holy Sepulchre stood almost in the centre of the walled city. Eleven years after the crucifixion, Golgotha was included within the perimeter of the city by a new wall built in the year 44 A.D. by Herod Agrippa. In the middle of the last century, remains of the ancient wall of the city were found to the east and north of the church in the neighbouring Russian Hospice. The Jewish tombs seen inside the church are also strong evidence that this district was outside the city, for, according to Jewish law, nobody can be buried within the precincts of the Holy City. The site of the crucifixion must have been venerated by the first Christians for the following reason. In 135 A.D., Hadrian, wanting to root out every remembrance of the Jewish religion and the Christian religion as a Jewish sect, obliterated Calvary and the tomb of Jesus by building a Roman temple dedicated to Jupiter. (The same was done in Bethlehem over the birthplace of Jesus). This act of hatred had a contrary result for instead of desecrating the place, he marked the site and preserved it until its triumphant discovery two centuries later by Constantine. In 326, Hadrian's temple was demolished by Queen Helena, Calvary and the tomb were found intact in accordance with Gospel reports. By order of Constantine, and under the supervision of his mother Helena, a magnificent basilica was erected over Calvary and the tomb. This grandiose monument of Constantine was destroyed in 614 by the Persians; rebuilt on a reduced scale by Abbot Modestos; it was again destroyed by the Khalif Hakem in 1009. The destruction of the church was the main reason that led to the Crusades. The church was restored in 1048 by Constantine Monomochus. The Crusaders, after the conquest of Jerusalem, erected in 1149 the church which is still standing. Despite the different additions and restorations, the church exists to this day in its main original outline. The church is divided between six communities under a Status Quo decreed by the Turkish rulers in 1852.

And when they were come to the place of a Skull, there they crucified.

Luke 23:33

CALVARY

was a large rock rising about 45 feet out of the ground. Its name (Place of the Skull) probably came from its appearance which resembles a skull. At present, there are two chapels at the top of Calvary — one is believed to be the site of the crucifixion and belongs to the Greek Orthodox, the second is believed to be the site where Jesus was stripped of his garments and nailed to the cross and belongs to the Roman Catholics. Approximately one third of the platform of the two chapels rests on the actual rock of Calvary. This rock can be seen under an altar dedicated to the Virgin Mary of Sorrows and below the inside of a chapel dedicated to Adam.

THE TOMB OF CHRIST

"Now there was in the place where he was crucified a garden; and in the garden a new sepulchre, wherein nobody had yet been laid. Because of the preparation of the Passover they laid Jesus, because the sepulchre was nigh at hand." (John 19:42) Jesus was laid in a tomb at the foot of Calvary. This tomb, hewn out of the rock, was made by Joseph of Arimathea's family. Joseph of Arimathea "who was a member of the Sanhedrin" was a disciple of Jesus, but in secret, because he was afraid of the Jews (John 19:38). The tomb that Joseph of Arimathea made was the type made for rich Jews. It was composed of two chambers — the first served as a meeting place for the mourners and in the second the corpse was laid on a slab cut in the rock. The actual tomb of Jesus, which was isolated from the rest of the hill by Queen Helena, existed till the year 1009 when it was totally destroyed by the Khalif Hakem. The present monument, with a Moscovite cupola was built over the site in 1810 by the Greek Orthodox and the Russians. Inside, a marble slab marks the place where the body of Jesus was laid. It is believed that the original stone slab is beneath the one that is displayed.

THE CITADEL

"Tower of David." The citadel was built by Herod the Great as a royal palace and as the western defence of Jerusalem. It was protected by three huge towers. He named the three towers Phasael after his brother, Hippicus after his friend and Mariame after his wife whom he murdered. This magnificent fortress-palace was spared by Titus in 70 A.D. to be used as barracks for the Tenth Roman Legion and as a witness to the heroism and might of the Roman soldiers. The massive Herodian blocks are still visible at the base. The citadel was restored by the Crusaders and the Mamelukes in the 12th and 14th century. Most of the present structure dates from the time of Suleiman the Magnificent who restored it in 1540. The citadel is also known as the Tower of David, as it is said that Herod built his palace on the site of an earlier fortress built by King David. At present, during the summer months, a sound and light production entitled "A Stone in David's Tower" is given at the Citadel.

The Old City Wall
Jaffa Gate and the Citadel

MOUNT MORIAH, THE "TEMPLE MOUNT"

He said, "Take now thy son, thine only one, Isaac, whom thou lovest, and go to the land of Moriah."

Genesis 22:2

is revered by the three great monotheistic faiths. For the Jews it is the ground where the great Temple stood; for the Christians it is associated with many events of Jesus' life and for the Moslems it is the third most sacred place after Mecca and Medina.

The history of Mount Moriah begins with Abraham. Tradition has identified it with the mount upon which Abraham had prepared to sacrifice his son Isaac (Genesis 22:1–22). Toward the end of his reign, David bought the bare hill top of this Mount which Araunah the Jebusite had used as a threshing floor (Samuel 24:18–25) and built an altar unto the Lord. David promised to build a temple to God but this honour was kept for his son, Solomon. Solomon built a magnificent temple and furnished it with precious imported wood, copper and gold vessels. The splendid temple that Solomon built was destroyed by Nebuchadnezzar in 587 B.C. and the Jews were taken captive into Babylon. Fifty years later, they returned from captivity and the Temple, on a smaller scale, was rebuilt by Zerubabel. Herod the Great, wishing to have his crimes forgotten and to render himself popular with the Jews, reconstructed the Temple on a large scale. Ten thousand workers were employed in this grandiose work, and the Temple, rebuilt with a double esplanade, regained its primitive splendour and beauty. The construction began in 20 B.C. and was not finished until 64 A.D., six years before its destruction. Herod's Temple was the one Jesus knew. In 70 A.D. the Temple was razed to the ground by the armies of Titus. Titus tried to spare the Temple which was one of the world's marvels, but his soldiers threw a lighted torch through a window and set it on fire. The Menorah, the seven branched candlestick was saved and carried with Titus in triumph back to Rome. In 135 A.D. after the crushing of the second Jewish revolt, Hadrian profaned the site by erecting a temple dedicated to Jupiter. The early Christians looked on Mount Moriah as a place cursed by God and the Mount became a heap of rubble. When, in 636 A.D. the Moslems conquered Jerusalem, the rubble was cleared from the Mount and the Khalif Omar built a mosque on the site, identifying it as the place where the prophet Mohammed went to heaven on his winged steed. In 691 Abed El Malik Ben Marwan, the Omayad Khalif, replaced the small mosque of Omar with the present one.

The Dome of the Rock, which ranks in sanctity after that of the Kaaba in Mecca and the tomb of the Prophet in Medina, is one of the most beautiful mosques of the Islamic world. During the past 13 centuries, the Dome of the Rock has been repaired many times but its outline remains the same as

Stained glass window

The Dome of the Rock (Interior)

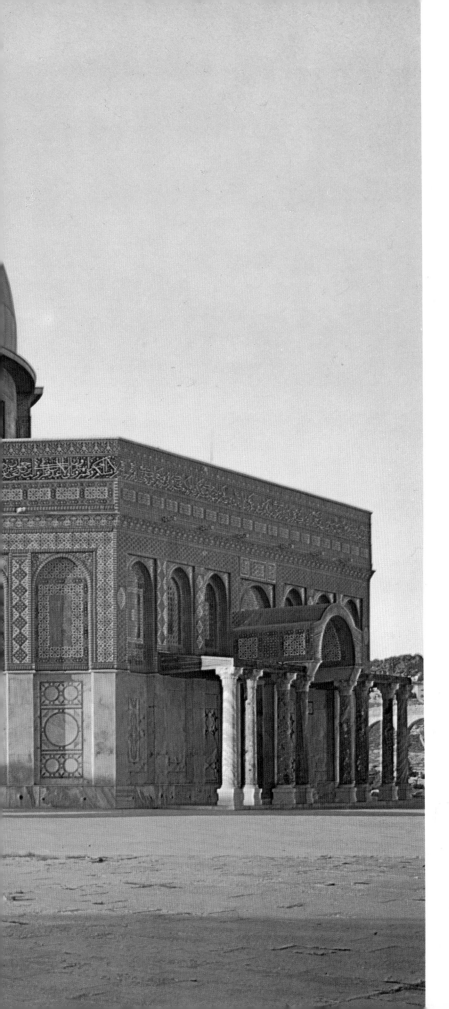

it was in 691. When the Crusaders conquered Jerusalem in 1099, the mosque was converted into the church of Templum Domini. After the defeat of the Crusaders at the Horns of Hittin in 1187, the cross which shone for 88 years above the dome was removed, and the crescent rose again in its place. Since that time, the Dome of the Rock has been a Moslem shrine. The Dome of the Rock, which is one of the oldest and most beautiful of Moslem shrines is the most exquisite and most striking monument in Jerusalem. Its design is Byzantine as it was built by Byzantine artists, but all of its decorations are Oriental. The exterior is a regular octagon, each side measuring 63 feet with a diameter of 180 feet. Above it rises a dome to a height of 108 feet from the ground and with a diameter of 78 feet. The octagonal structure is encased in marble slabs up to 18 feet high and above that, to the upper edge, the walls are decorated with brilliant Persian tiles. The dome is made of plates of aluminium impregnated with gold which gleam in the brilliant sunshine.

THE ROCK OF

MOUNT MORIAH

Beneath the dome of this magnificent building lies the rock of Mount Moriah. It is 15 yards long, 12 yards wide and rises to a height of 2 yards above the ground. This is the traditional rock where Abraham prepared to sacrifice his son, Isaac. Moslems believe that Abraham took his son Ishmael, to sacrifice and not Isaac. They also believe that the prophet Mohammed ascended to heaven in a night journey from this rock. During the period of the Crusaders, the rock was surrounded by an iron screen to prevent pilgrims from taking pieces and selling them as souvenirs. The iron screen was replaced in 1959 by a wooden balustrade. The interior of the building, with the beautifully decorated cupola, the richly coloured stained glass windows and the lovely mosaic of the walls, offer a charming variety of colours and an enchanting atmosphere for worship.

(The distant Mosque) at the southern part of the esplanade, was built between 709–715 by Khalif Waleed, son of Abed El Malik who built the Dome of the Rock. Very little of the original remains in the present structure as it has been destroyed and renovated many times. The Mosque stands almost on the site of Solomon's palace and was built on the foundation of a Byzantine church. During the Crusader's occupation of Jerusalem, El Aksa served first as the palace of the Latin Kings and later was converted into the headquarters of the knights of the Templars. The El Aksa Mosque is used for group prayers while the Dome of the Rock is used for individual worship.

EL AKSA

SOLOMON'S STABLES

When Herod the Great rebuilt the Temple, he doubled the surface of the esplanade by adding a plat-form supported by a series of huge arches and pillars at the southeast corner. This subterranean struc-ture is known as Solomon's Stables. It is not known if these vaults were used as stables by Herod, but it is historically certain that they were used as stables by the Crusaders. Holes made in the stones for tethering the horses can still be seen.

THE EXCAVATIONS

Since the beginning of the excavations in 1968, man
tons of rubble have been removed and careful
examined. Ivory, bronze figurines and a veritab
treasury of coins of different periods have been foun
Many details of earlier structures were uncovere
Excavations have revealed the remains of an eno
mous right-angled stairway that led to the Temp
mount from the South. The uppermost arch is still v
sible, jutting out of the Western Wall near its southe
extremity. It is named "Robinson's Arch" after t
explorer who discovered it.

THE WESTERN WALL

(Wailing Wall) is the holiest shrine of the Jewish world. It is revered as the last relic of the last Temple. The Western Wall is a portion of the retaining wall that Herod built around the second Temple in 20 B.C. Titus, in the year 70 A.D., spared this part of the wall with its huge blocks to show future generations the greatness of the Roman soldiers who had been able to destroy the rest of the building. During the Roman period, Jews were not allowed to come to Jerusalem. However, during the Byzantine period, they were allowed to come once a year on the anniversary of the destruction of the Temple to lament the dispersion of their people and weep over the ruins of the Holy Temple, which is why this section of the wall became known as the Wailing Wall. The custom of praying at the wall continued for centuries. From 1948–1967 Jews were not allowed to visit the wall as it was in the Jordanian section of the city. After the Six Day War, the Wailing Wall became a place for national rejoicing as well as a place of worship. A large esplanade was cleared to accommodate thousands of worshippers.

THE MOUNT OF OLIVES

is located east of Jerusalem, across the Kidron Valley. Its summit, which is about 300 feet higher than Jerusalem, offers a magnificent view of the Old City and a striking panorama of the Judean Hills as far as the Dead Sea and the mountains of Moab in the east. The Mount of Olives is venerated by Jews and Christians. For Jews, the prophets Haggai, Zechariah and Malachi are buried here. For the Christians, it is associated with some of the most important events in the life of Christ. Here Christ ascended to heaven, foretold the destruction of Jerusalem and taught his disciples the sublime Lord's prayer. Here Christ often came for meditation and prayer, and probably spent the nights under the trees or in the caves, as it was not safe for him in Jerusalem.

THE GARDEN
OF GETHSEMANE

is one of the most impressive sites in the Holy Land. It lies at the foot of the Mount of Olives. It appears today as it was twenty centuries ago. On the opposite hill across the Kidron Valley, city followed city, but this garden is still kept almost as it was at the time of Jesus maybe with the same olive trees. St. John spoke of it as a garden over the Kidron brook. It was a spot favoured by Jesus "It was a place where Jesus often went for His retreat and prayer" (Luke 22:39). This is the garden where Jesus on His last night underwent the most sorrowful hour of His passion, the hour in which He trembled in His nature, choosing to suffer and die on the cross, taking upon Himself the sins of all mankind. "Father, if thou be willing, remove this cup from me, nevertheless not my will, but thine be done." (Luke 24:42). Judas came then with the servants of the high priest and betrayed his master (Matthew 26:47, Mark 14:44, Luke 22:47, John 18:2, 3). All the disciples fled, leaving him alone, fulfilling the prophecy which says "I shall smite the shepherd and the sheep will be scattered." Jesus was arrested, taken to the house of Caiphas and condemned the following day to death on the cross. In the Garden of Gethsemane, there are eight olive trees whose age is lost in antiquity. Some botanists claim that they may be

3,000 years old. Josephus relates that Titus cut down all trees in the environs of Jerusalem in 70 A.D. If these trees escaped destruction, they are the very contemporaries of Christ as they are Roman olive trees. If not, they are without doubt the shoots of those under which Jesus prayed that night of His agony. "The olive tree does not die." (Pliny). They still bear fruit.

THE CHURCH OF GETHSEMANE

"Father, if thou, art willing, remove this cup from me, nevertheless not my will, but thine, be done."

Luke 22:42

In 379 the Byzantines built the first basilica over the place made holy by the prayer and Agony of Christ. This basilica was one of the first to be destroyed in 614 by the Persians. In the 12th century the Crusaders rebuilt the church which was later destroyed. The present church, which is one of Jerusalem's most beautiful, was built in 1919–1924. Since sixteen nations contributed to its construction, it was called the "Church of all Nations." The coat of arms of each contributing nation is to be seen in the cupolas and pictures. All the cupolas are decorated with beautiful mosaics and the magnificent windows are of translucent alabaster. The dim light filtering through the purple windows and the beauty of the interior, make a lovely atmosphere for prayer and meditation. Part of the traditional rock of agony lies in front of the main altar. A section of the mosaic floor of the Byzantine church was discovered and the new mosaic floor is an exact copy of the original. On the brilliant facade are the statues of the four Evangelists, each holding a book with an inscription. In the pediment is a magnificent mosaic representing Christ offering His and the world's suffering to His Father.

Basilica of Agony

"Hosanna to the son of David... Hosanna in the highest...
Matthew 21:9

THE CHAPEL OF THE ASCENSION

The Acts (1:9–12) tell how Jesus took his disciples to a mount called Olivet and how, after blessing them, he ascended to heaven. The top of the Mount of Olives is considered to be the site of the Ascension. In the Acts it is said that the disciples departed from the Mount of Olives which was a Sabbath day's journey away from Jerusalem. A Sabbath day's journey is about 1000 yards and this is approximately the distance which separates the site of the Ascension from Jerusalem.

A Byzantine church was built on the site in the 4th century and was destroyed by the Persians in 614. The Crusaders built another church in the 12th century. The present small chapel is an edifice built by the Crusaders in the court of their curch to contain the rock, with the legendary footprint of Christ, made when he ascended to heaven. The Moslems, who still occupy the site, walled the arcades and added the present cupola.

THE PATER NOSTER

The church of the Pater Noster is built on the traditional site where Jesus taught his disciples the Lord's Prayer, foretold the terrible destruction of Jerusalem and revealed his last coming and the end of the world (Matthew 24:1–3, Luke 21:5–7). Constantine, who honoured the cave of the Nativity in Bethlehem and the tomb of Christ in Jerusalem with magnificent buildings, built a church on the top of the Mount of Olives to commemorate the words of Jesus concerning the destruction of Jerusalem and His last coming. Constantine's church was destroyed in 614 by the Persians and rebuilt in the 12th century by the Crusaders. After the defeat of the Crusaders, the church was destroyed and the site was occupied by Moslems. In 1868 Princess Aurelia de Bossi de la Tour d'Auvergne bought the site and donated it to France. In 1875 she built a convent for the order of the Carmelite nuns. Inside the church and on the walls of the cloister, the Lord's Prayer is written in 62 languages. The Princess Aurelia de Bossi is buried in the cloister. Excavations carried out in 1910–1911 revealed the remains of the previous churches. In 1918 France organized a subscription for a world basilica in honour of the Sacred Heart, began the work but failed to complete it.

THE TOMB
OF THE VIRGIN
MARY

The blessed Virgin died in Jerusalem, and according to tradition, was buried in the Kidron Valley. The present church was built by the Crusaders over the ruins of a Byzantine basilica. The site marks the traditional place of her tomb and her Assumption. The Assumption of Mary was defined as a Catholic article of faith in 1950. Control of the church passed from the hands of the Franciscans to the Greeks and Armenians in 1757. The Syrians, Copts, and Abyssinians have minor rights. Moslems have the right to worship in this shrine.

THE
RUSSIAN CHURCH

The Russian church of St. Mary Magdalene with its 7 striking onion shaped spires, is a fine example of old Moscovite church style. It was built in 1888 by Czar Alexander III in memory of his mother and named after Saint Mary Magdalene. It is maintained by the white Russian nuns. In the crypt lies the body of the Grand Duchess Elizabeth Feodronova, sister of the Empress Alexandra. She was killed in 1918 in Siberia by the Bolsheviks — and in accordance with her wishes her body was brought to Jerusalem for burial.

DOMINUS FLEVIT

"The Lord Wept." During His triumphal entry into Jerusalem on Palm Sunday, Jesus, seeing the city, halted and wept over it. (Luke 19:37–42) The site of Christ's weeping over Jerusalem was only marked in the 12th century by the Crusaders who erected a church which fell into ruins after their withdrawal. The present church, built in 1891, was designed to resemble a tear shaped shrine. The altar is framed by a panoramic glass window facing Jerusalem.

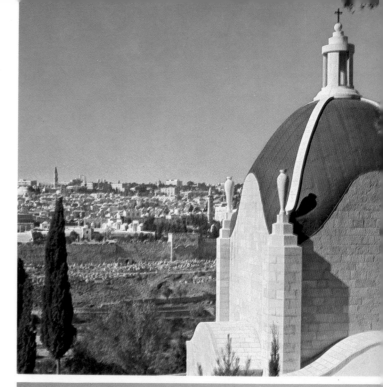

THE JEWISH CEMETERY

On the slopes of the Mount of Olives is the oldest and largest Jewish cemetery in the world. Many Jews came to Jerusalem in order to die and be buried near the Valley of Jehoshaphat where it is believed the resurrection and final judgement will take place (Joel 4:1–2). Christians and Moslems share the same belief and their graves are situated on the western side of the valley.

THE KIDRON VALLEY

The Kidron Valley separates the Mt. of Olives from the City of Jerusalem. This Valley had been crossed by Jesus many times, either going to the Temple through the Golden Gate or ascending to the Mt. of Olives where he used

to spend the night at Gethsemane, or at Bethany in the house of his friend Lazarus. He surely crossed this valley on the memorable evening of Holy Thursday, when, leaving the cenacle, he went with his disciples to Gethsemane, and again after he was betrayed and led to the house of the High Priest Caiphas. In the Kidron Valley there are four ancient tombs which are taken for the tombs of Absalom, Jehoshaphat, St. James and St. Zacharias. The architectural style of these tombs show that they belong to an earlier period which is the Hellenistic period, and were probably erected by private families. According to local tradition, the Kidron will be the site of the last Divine Judgement. This belief has made the Kidron Valley a huge necropolis in which Jews, Moslems and Christians alike choose to be buried.

HEZEKIAH'S TUNNEL

In the year 700 B.C., Hezekiah, king of Jerusalem, in order to protect the water supply of his city from the invading Assyrians, cut a tunnel in the solid rock. This was to channel the water of the Gihon spring, located outside the walled city, into the pool of Siloam which was within the walls of the city. The outlet was closed and hidden from the eyes of the invaders. Jerusalem was saved since the Assyrian army, brought low by thirst, failed to conquer the city and withdrew. The roughly "S" shaped tunnel is 600 yards long. The workmen began tunneling at each end and accomplished the remarkable engineering feat of meeting in the middle within 4 feet of each other. The workmen recorded their joyous meeting by an inscription which was found in 1880. The inscription, written in old Hebrew, tells how working from opposite ends, the two groups of workmen managed to meet. The inscription was taken to the Istanbul Museum. The Gihon fountain, also called the fountain of the Virgin, is one of Jerusalem's earliest sources of water. The Jebusites used its water by means of a gallery leading to a shaft; this was the shaft through which David's commandos broke into the city and took it from the Jebusites. Solomon was crowned king at the Gihon spring (I Kings 1:33, 38, 45).

THE POOL OF SILOAM

This pool was probably costructed by King Hezekiah as a reservoir at the southern end of the tunnel to receive the water of the Gihon spring. The pool is sacred to the Christians as it was to this pool that Jesus sent the blind man to wash the clay from his eyes. "So he went and washed and came back seeing" (John 9). In the 5th century a church was built over the pool, but it was destroyed in 614 by the Persians and never rebuilt.

"Let the Children come to me, do not hinder them, for to such belongs the Kingdom of God".

Mark 10:14

Religious ceremony of the oriental Christian communities of Jerusalem. The Greek Orthodox, the Armenians, the Assyrians, the Copts, the Abyssinians.

View of the site of David's City prior to the establishment of Jerusalem. The picture shows the South Wall of the Old City, Mount Zion with the Dormition Abbey and St. Peter in Gallicantu with part of the village of Siloan.

Model of the city of Jerusalem of Herod's time. The topography is an exact copy of Jerusalem during the time of Christ. It is located in the grounds of the Holyland Hotel, Jerusalem.

THE LAST SUPPER ROOM

(Coenaculum, Dining Hall) is the place where Jesus ate the Last Supper with his disciples, establishing the communion service (Mark 14:12–16, Luke 22:7–13). In the same room Jesus appeared twice to His disciples after His resurrection (John 20:19–23, 22, 24, 29). In this same room the disciples received the Holy Ghost (Acts 2:1–4). The first Christians had their headquarters on Mount Zion, and as early as the 1st century a church was built here. This church escaped destruction in the year 70 A.D. and again in 135 A.D. as it was outside the area of military operations. It was enlarged by the Byzantines and called "Holy Zion" to associate the first Christian church with the prophecy of Isaiah "For out of Zion shall go forth the law and the word of the Lord from Jerusalem." It was probably from this shrine that the mount received its name. In 614 the Persians destroyed the church and the Crusaders rebuilt it in the 12th century as two separate superimposed chapels, as it is today. In 1176 King David's Tomb was located in the lower chapel and in 1552 the Christians were expelled by the Turks from the upper chapel which was converted into a mosque by simply adding a minaret and a prayer niche—Mihrab.

THE BASILICA OF THE DORMITION

is the most imposing building on Mount Zion. It marks the site where the Virgin Mary died. In 1100 the Crusaders built a large church and called it St. Mary of Mount Zion. It was destroyed in 1219 by the Moslems who occupied the site. In 1898 the site was given by the Turks to the German Emperor Wilhelm II. The Emperor gave the land to the Benedictine Fathers who built the present church in 1910. The apse of the church is decorated with a beautiful mosaic of Mary and the Child. The floor mosaic has symbols of the Trinity, representations of the apostles and the signs of the Zodiac. In the crypt is a stone effigy of the Virgin Mary asleep on her deathbed.

MOUNT ZION

Mount Zion rises to the southwest of the old, walled city. It was once within the walls of ancient Jerusalem. It is sacred to the Christians, Jews and Moslems. For Christians, it is the site of the Last Supper and the place where the Virgin Mary died. For the Jews and Moslems it contains the reputed tomb of King David, who is venerated by both.

"For out of Zion shall go forth the law and the word of the Lord from Jerusalem."
Isaiah 2:3

THE TOMB OF KING DAVID

This is one of the most sacred Jewish sites in Israel, second only to the Western Wall. The tomb was described and located here by Rabbi Benjamin of Tudela when he visited Jerusalem in 1172. It is made of stone, covered with an embroidered cloth and embellished with silver crowns of the Torah.

ST. PETER IN GALLICANTU

"And Peter remembered the word of the Lord, "Before the cock crows to-day, you will deny me three times" And he went out and wept bitterly.
Luke 22:61:62

"Cock-crow". This church overlooking the Kidron valley was built by the Assumptionist Fathers in 1931 over the traditional site of the house of the high priest Caiphas. Jesus, betrayed and arrested in the garden of Gethsemane, was brought to this house. Here He spent the entire night and this was the scene of His first trial (Matthew 26:57–63, Mark 14:53–65, Luke 22:63–71, John 18:12–14). Here St. Peter wept at the crowing of the cock in fulfilment of Christ's words. He denied his Lord three times before the cock had crowed twice (Matthew 26:34, Mark 14:66–72, Luke 22:54–62, John 18:15–18). As a result of excavations, the Assumptionist Fathers are convinced that their church stands on the site of Caiphas' house. An almost complete set of Hebrew measures, a stone mill, a dungeon, a courtyard, servants' quarters and remains of a Byzantine church were discovered. On the left side of the church, a flight of ancient steps was discovered. These steps in the hillside are believed to date from the time of Christ. As this is the shortest way from Gethsemane to the upper city, it is very possible that the feet of Jesus trod these very stones. At the time of Jesus, the site was within the walls of Jerusalem.

THE TOMB
THEN TOOK THEY THE BODY OF JESUS, AND WOUND IT IN LINEN
CLOTHES WITH THE SPICES, AS THE MANNER OF THE JEWS IS TO BURY.
NOW IN THE PLACE WHERE HE WAS CRUCIFIED THERE WAS A GARDEN;
AND IN THE GARDEN A NEW SEPULCHRE, WHEREIN WAS NEVER MAN
YET LAID.
THERE LAID THEY JESUS THEREFORE BECAUSE OF THE
JEWS' PREPARATION DAY; FOR THE SEPULCHRE WAS NIGH
AT HAND.
John 19: 40-42

ויקחו את גופת ישוע ויעטוה בתכריכים אשר מלאו בשמים כדרך קבורת היהודים:
ובמקום אשר נצלב שם היה גן וגן קבר חדש אשר עוד לא נקבר בו א'ש: ובהיות
היום ערב שבת ליהודים והקבר קרוב קברו בו את ישוע:
יוחנן 19: 40-42

TO MNHMEION
EΛΑΒΟΝ ΟΥΝ ΤΟ ΣΩΜΑ ΤΟΥ ΙΗΣΟΥ ΚΑΙ ΕΔΗΣΑΝ ΑΥΤΟ ΟΘΟΝΙΟΙΣ
ΜΕΤΑ ΤΩΝ ΑΡΩΜΑΤΩΝ, ΚΑΘΩΣ ΕΘΟΣ ΕΣΤΙ ΤΟΙΣ ΙΟΥΔΑΙΟΙΣ ΕΝΤΑΦΙΑΖΕΙΝ.
ΗΝ ΔΕ ΕΝ ΤΩ ΤΟΠΩ ΟΠΟΥ ΕΣΤΑΥΡΩΘΗ ΚΗΠΟΣ, ΚΑΙ ΕΝ ΤΩ ΚΗΠΩ
ΜΝΗΜΕΙΟΝ ΚΑΙΝΟΝ, ΕΝ Ω ΟΥΔΕΠΩ ΟΥΔΕΙΣ ΕΤΕΘΗ.
ΕΚΕΙ ΟΥΝ ΔΙΑ ΤΗΝ ΠΑΡΑΣΚΕΥΗΝ ΤΩΝ ΙΟΥΔΑΙΩΝ, ΟΤΙ ΕΓΓΥΣ
ΗΝ ΤΟ ΜΝΗΜΕΙΟΝ, ΕΘΗΚΑΝ ΤΟΝ ΙΗΣΟΥΝ.
Ἰωάννης 19: 40-42

Gordon's Calvary

Golgotha

THE ~~ARDEN~~ TOMB

The site north of the Damascus Gate is believed by many to be the place of Crucifixion and Resurrection of Jesus Christ.

In 1883, the British General Charles Gordon noted this rocky hill which resembled a human skull, and suggested that this might be the true Calvary. The presence of a nearby rock-hewn tomb, believed to be first century, helped to strengthen this idea, and the scriptural significance of the site appealed to many eminent Christians of that day.

An Association was formed, and by 1892, sufficient money was collected to purchase the tomb and its surroundings, and have it cared for by a resident warden. The Garden Tomb gives a clear picture of what the place of Crucifixion and burial of Christ must have looked like at the time of Jesus. The simplicity and beauty of the site and the peaceful atmosphere of The Garden Tomb, make it a favourable spot for prayer and meditation.

MEA SHEARIM

This quarter, which is the stronghold of the Jewish Orthodoxy in Jerusalem, was established in 1875. It is inhabited by eastern European Jews who have retained the mode of life practised and garments worn in the ghettos of Europe. They walk around oblivious to the secular world around them. The Hassidic Jews spend much of their lives in the numerous small prayer houses, synagogues and yeshivas, for this quarter is blessed with many synagogues and schools for the learning of the Torah and its commentaries.

THE SHRINE OF THE BOOK

This small museum, an onion-top shaped building, is designed to resemble the lids of the jars in which the Dead Sea Scrolls were discovered. The Essene Community considered themselves as the Sons of Light and the rest of the world as the Sons of Darkness. This concept is expressed by the contrast between the whiteness of the Shrine and the blackness of the wall near the entrance. The black marble wall is also supposed to recall the heavy burden which lay on Israel for 2,000 years. The shrine, symbolizing a cave, is a subterranean building with a tunnel-shaped interior. It houses the famous Dead Sea Scrolls, scrolls found at Masada, the Bar Kokhba letters and objects found at the sites of the discoveries.

THE
KNESSET

The "Parliament Building" is a $7,000,000 building constructed with the red stones of Jerusalem. It was established with funds from the family of James de Rothschild in England and was inaugurated in 1966. It contains all kinds of facilities including an excellent library of over 50,000 volumes. The wrought iron entrance to the Knesset is the work of the famous Israeli sculptor, Polombo. The 16 foot high Menorah (7 branched candelabrum), symbol of the State of Israel, stands opposite the entrance. It depicts scenes from Jewish history and was donated by the British Parliament. The Israeli Parliament is composed of 120 members elected by a general vote of all citizens over the age of eighteen. Elections take place every four years.

CHAGALL
WINDOWS

A small synagogue at the Hadassah Hospital houses the twelve world famous stained glass windows of Marc Chagall, representing the twelve tribes of Israel and their symbols as described in the Torah.

BETHLEHEM

"For to you is born this day in the city of David a Saviour who is Christ the Lord."

Luke 2:11

(House of bread in Hebrew and house of meat in Arabic) lies five miles south of Jerusalem on a hill about 2,600 feet above sea level. It has a population of about 30,000. Few people work the fertile terraces on the hillsides, a good number make religious objects for pilgrims, mainly from olive wood and mother of pearl. The mother of pearl industry was introduced into Bethlehem at the time of the Crusaders. Bethlehem's history goes deep into the past and its record goes back to the very remote times of the patriarchs. It was mentioned in the Bible in connection with the death of Rachel. "Rachel began to be in labour and to suffer great distress with her last breath, for she was at the point of death. She called her son Ben Oni, his father however, named him Benjamin. Thus Rachel died and she was buried on the road to Ephrata that is Bethlehem (Genesis 35:16–18, 19). Bethlehem was the scene of the idyll of Ruth the Moabite and Boaz. Elimelech

Bethlehem, Market Scene

and his wife Naomi went to Moab with their two sons at the time of a famine (Ruth 1:1). After the death of her husband and two sons, Naomi, with Ruth her daughter-in-law, returned to Bethlehem (Ruth 1:19—22). In Bethlehem Ruth met Boaz and married him. She was to be the great-grandmother of David and thus Bethlehem was the original house of the family of David. For this reason, Joseph, who was from the branch of David, came to Bethlehem to be registered. In Bethlehem David was born and here he spent his childhood herding the flocks over the hilly wilderness of Judah. Here he was called and anointed King of Israel by the prophet Samuel (I Samuel 16:1—4). The event which rendered the little town of Bethlehem immortal was the birth of Jesus in one of its caves. 750 years before the birth of Christ, the prophet Micah wrote "But you Bethlehem Ephrata, the least of the clans of Judah, out of you will be born for me the one who is to rule over Israel (Micah 5:1—2). This prophecy was fulfilled when a decree of Caesar Augustus commanding a census of all the provinces subject to the Roman Empire, brought Mary and Joseph from Nazareth to their native city. "So Joseph set out from the town of Nazareth in Galilee and travelled up to Judea, to the town of David called Bethlehem, since he was of David's house and line, in order to be registered together with Mary his betrothed who was with child. While they were there, the time came for her to have her child, and she gave birth to a son, her first born. She wrapped him in swaddling clothes, and laid him in a manger because there was no room for them at the inn (Luke 2:1—20). Since that event, which marked the transition between the Old Testament and the New, Bethlehem won eternal renown, becoming sacred and dear to the hearts of millions of Christians. In Bethlehem there are a number of old houses built over caves in the lime stone. These caves are old and similar to the cave of the Nativity. Probably Jesus was born in one of these old caves rather than in the stable of western tradition. In the year 135 A.D., Hadrian, after crushing the second Jewish revolt, profaned the town of Bethlehem as well as Jerusalem by bringing into them the worship of false gods. In Bethlehem he completely surrounded the cave of the Nativity by a temple dedicated to Adonis, god of beauty and love. This providential desecration of the cave served to fix the site for the future. Hadrian's temple stood above the cave for two centuries until its destruction by Queen Helena, the mother of the Emperor Constantine, who, in 313 was converted and proclaimed Christianity to be the official religion of the Roman Empire. In 325, Helena, Constantine's mother, visited the Holy Land and built three basilicas, the first over Calvary and the tomb of Christ in Jerusalem, the second over the cave of the Nativity in Bethlehem and the third one on the top of the Mount of Olives. In Bethlehem, as in Jerusalem, there was no problem in locating the correct place. Identification was based on documentary evidence and Christian tradition which passed from father to son. Christian tradition pointed out the cave where Jesus was born at the eastern end of the village beneath the temple of Hadrian. The temple was removed and the cave was found intact. Constantine then built a magnificent basilica very richly decorated with mosaic, marble and frescoes. He honoured the church with royal offerings of gold, silver and embroidered tapestries as he was particularly interested that the church of the Nativity should be a memorial to his mother's piety. In 529 the Samaritans from Nablus revolted against the Christian Byzantine government and plundered the countryside and Bethlehem. The church of the Nativity was badly damaged, looted and burned. The mosaic floors of the Constantine church, recently discovered, were found to be covered with thick layers of ashes and burnt tiles. The Patriarch of Jerusalem sent St. Sabbas to Emperor Justinian to ask for his help in restoring the church. The Emperor sent an envoy with vast funds and wrote to the agent of Palestine to hand over the revenues of the country to his envoy so that he could build a larger and more beautiful church. The Emperor was not satisfied with the work, accused his envoy of having pocketed the money and had him beheaded. The Justinian church is the one still standing and which we see today in Bethlehem. In spite of the fact that all the interior beauty was damaged through the centuries, the essential form has not altered. In 614 the Persians invaded the Holy Land and destroyed all its churches and convents; according to some historians, they destroyed more than 300 churches and convents. The church of the Nativity was the only church which evaded destruction. A mosaic scene of the Nativity representing the Wise Men in ancient Persian costumes worshipping the Child, deterred them from their vandalistic purpose. During the time of the Crusaders, the church was in need of repair and restoration was effected for most of it. Old floor marbles were replaced, the roof of cedar was covered with lead, the side walls were covered with marble and the upper part of the nave was covered with splendid mosaics. In the year 1100 on Christmas Day, Baldwin, the first king of the Latin Kingdom, was crowned in the church of Bethlehem. He refused to be crowned with a gold crown in Jerusalem, where Christ had been crowned with thorns. His successor, Baldwin the second, was also crowned here in 1109.

THE FACADE OF THE CHURCH OF THE NATIVITY

The outside aspect is austere and resembles a mediaeval fortress. The facade is now encircled by the walls of three convents. It originally had three doors, two of which were walled up; of the middle one there remains a low narrow entrance which gives onto the church. This entrance was lowered twice to prevent marauders from entering the church with their horses. The original cornice and the pointed arch of the Crusader church can be distinguished.

INTERIOR OF THE CHURCH

The basilica has the shape of a cross 170 feet long and 80 feet wide. It is divided into five aisles by four rows of columns which are of the red stone of the country. Fragments of mosaics from the 4th century church were discovered in 1936. They are covered with a wooden floor. On the upper part of the church and transept walls, mosaic fragments can be seen and they are all that is left of the Crusader wall decoration. The beautiful Greek orthodox choir stall standing above the cave of the Nativity is hand carved wood from cedars of Lebanon.

THE GROTTO OF THE NATIVITY

"She gave birth to her first born son and wrapped him ... laid him in a manger because there was no place for them in the inn."
Luke 2:7

Two entrances lead down to the rectangular shaped cave, 35 feet by 10 feet in size. It is lit by 48 lamps. A silver star with the Latin inscription "Hic de Maria Virgine Jesus Christus Natus est" (Here Christ was born) marks the spot where Christ was born. The Holy Manger lies to the right. The primitive rock, blackened by the smoke of candles and lamps, may be seen above the manger. The original roof of the cave was replaced by masonry in the fourth century. The walls of the grotto are covered with asbestos, a safeguard against fire and donated in 1874 by MacMahon, President of the French Republic.

THE "STAR"

In the Grotto, under the central altar, is a silver star commemorating the "Nativity", the birth of Christ. Christian tradition, and art in all its forms is inextricably linked with the star. Indeed, St. Matthew's Gospel, recalling the visit of the Magi to Bethlehem, says: "...We have seen His star in the East and have come to worship Him... And lo, the star went before them, till it came over the place where the Child was." (2/1—13).

THE SHEPHERDS' FIELD

And in that region there were shepherds out in the field keeping watch over their flock by night."
Luke 2:8

"And there was in the same country shepherds watching and keeping the night watches over their flocks, and behold an angel of the Lord stood by them, and the brightness of God shone round about them. Fear not for behold I bring you good tidings of great joy, for this day is born to you a Saviour, who is Christ the Lord." (Luke 2). Although the gospel words do not localize the exact place where the shepherds were, the ancient tradition has fixed the site in a field some 2 miles east of Bethlehem.

RACHEL'S TOMB

Rachel died and was buried on the way to Ephrata, that is Bethlehem. Jacob erected a memorial over her grave and this memorial marks Rachel's grave to this day. (Genesis 35:16–20). The small domed monument over the tomb dates from the 15th century. The tomb is sacred to Jews, Moslems and Christians. Women of the area visit the tomb and often pray for fertility and successful childbirth.

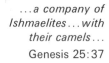

A WOMAN OF BETHLEHEM

The older generation of Bethlehem women still wear the traditional costume — a long black belted robe, and a white veil flowing down to the shoulders. A string of coins is attached to a red cone worn on the head. This type of dress was brought here by the Crusaders.

...a company of Ishmaelites...with their camels...
Genesis 25:37

HERODIUM

With its conical summit resembling a volcano, the Herodium stands in the wilderness of Judea 5 miles south-east of Bethlehem. Climbing to the summit you find that the "crater" is man-made and in its cup lie the ruins of a magnificent fortified palace which was built by Herod the Great.

Round the base were royal apartments, terraced gardens, pools, and 200 steps of the purest white marble led to the citadel on the top. Josephus, describing the Herodium wrote "Though meant only as a residence for a king, by the great number of structures, variety of conveniences, splendour and extent of the whole, the palace had the appearance of a city rather than a castle". Herod died in Jericho but he was buried here in a bier which was of solid gold studded with precious stones.

The Herodium has now been excavated by Fr. V. Corbo with financial aid from the Italian government. During four campaigns, (1962–1967) all of the outer perimeter of the fortress and some of the towers, plus the baths have been revealed. There is as yet no trace of Herod's tomb.

And the Lord appeared unto him in the plains of Mamre, and he sat in the tent door in the heat of the day.

Genesis 18:1

On your travels through the Holy Land you will see scenes of country life reminiscent of biblical times.

HEBRON

Hebron, 20 miles south of Jerusalem, stands at a height of 3,000 feet above sea level. The Hebron region is very hilly but the hillsides are well terraced and watered and the soil is rich. It is a good fruit growing district. The best grapes grown around Hebron come from the valley of Eshkol, the same valley from which the spies of Moses returned, "carrying great clusters of grapes between them on poles" (Numbers 13:23). Hebron, surrounded by beautiful orchards and gardens is famous for its industries of pottery, hand blown glass known as "Hebron glass" and sheepskin coats. Glass and pottery are still made in the same way as in ancient times. Hebron is one of the oldest cities in Palestine. According to the Bible, it was founded about the 17th century B.C. According to Dr. Hammond, Hebron is the oldest continuously occupied unwalled city in the world. Hebron entered history with Abraham. "After leaving his nephew Lot in the region of Bethel, Abraham moved his tent and came and dwelt by the oaks of Mamre which are at Hebron, and there he built an altar to the Lord." (Genesis 13:18). When his wife Sara died, Abraham spoke to the Hittites about buying a burial place for his wife. "I am a stranger and a sojourner among you, give me property among you for a burial place, that I may bury my dead out of my sight." (Genesis 23:4). After an oriental bargaining, Abraham bought the cave of Machpela for four hundred shekels of silver from Ephron the Hittite. (Genesis 23:8–16). The cave of Machpela became the family burial place where Sara, Abraham himself, Isaac, Rebecca, Leah and finally Jacob, whose body was brought from Egypt were buried. When David was proclaimed king, he made Hebron his capital for $7\frac{1}{2}$ years before he took Jerusalem and made it the capital of all Israel. Absalom, David's son, was born in Hebron and here he raised the standard of revolt against his father (IISamuel 15:10). During the Babylonian captivity, the city fell into the hands of the Idumeans who held it until it was recaptured by Judah Maccabeus. Before the destruction of Jerusalem by Titus, the city was captured and burned by the Roman general Cerealis. With the Moslem conquest of Palestine Hebron prospered and became the fourth sacred city of Islam, because of its association with Abraham, who is revered by the Moslems as the "Friend of God." In the 12th century, Hebron was taken by the Crusaders and became the seat of a Latin bishop. In 1187 it was retaken by Saladin. In 1517 it came under Turkish occupation for four centuries until the first world war when it was occupied by the allied armies in 1917. Hebron is one of the four sacred Jewish cities and since modern times it is a centre of Jewish learning.

Potter and Glass Blowers at work

THE MOSQUE OF ABRAHAM

I am a stranger and a sojourner among you, give me property among you for a burying place.
Genesis 23:4

Herod the Great, builder of the Temple in Jerusalem, was the first to build a beautiful temple over the cave of Machpela in Hebron. The foundations that he laid with large stones are still standing. Some of the stones are more than 20 feet long. Similar Herodian blocks are seen at the Western Wall in Jerusalem. Thus the outer walls with the large stones rising to a height of more than 40 feet are Herodian from the first century B.C. The upper parts of the wall are Byzantine, Crusader and Mameluke additions. The mosque, which occupies the southern part of the enclosure, was a Crusader church built over the remains of a Byzantine basilica. This huge rectangular building (200 feet long and 100 feet wide) began as a Jewish Temple built by Herod the Great. It was converted into a church in the 4th century by the Byzantines, into a mosque by the Moslems in the 7th century, into a church by the Crusaders and again into a mosque by Saladin.

THE TOMBS IN THE CAVE OF MACHPELA

The present structure of the mosque which stands over the cave of Machpela is mainly Crusader. In the mosque there are six tombs which are said to stand directly above the graves of the patriarchs and their wives buried in the cave. The Moslems never descend into the cave which is considered to be too sacred to walk in. The tombs of Abraham, Isaac and Jacob are covered with green and gold cloths and those of Sara, Rebecca and Leah with crimson cloths.

Tombs of Isaac and Rebecca

There, they buried Abraham and Sarah his wife; there they buried Isaac and Rebekah his wife; and there I buried Leah.

Genesis 49: 31

*We piped to you,
and you did not dance,
we wailed and you
did not mourn.*
Matthew 11:17

MAMRE

*Come to me, all who
labour and are heavy
laden, and I will
give you rest.*
Mathew 11:28

After separating from his nephew Lot, Abraham came to Mamre and built an altar to God. Here he received the three angels who announced to him that his wife Sara would have a son. (Genesis 18:10). From here Abraham went to rescue Lot (Genesis 14: 13—14). Here Abraham pleaded for Sodom and Gomorrah (Genesis 18:23—32). Here David was anointed King. Since the 7th century the site of Mamre was forgotten and many places claimed the honour of being the true Mamre. In 1926 a German society excavated Haram Ramat El Khalil (Enclosure of the High Place of the Friend) and found remains of the different buildings which had successively been built at Mamre (Herod's, Hadrian's, Byzantine and Arab). Thus this site became the accepted Mamre.

BETHANY

"And seeing a fig tree by the wayside he went to it, and found nothing on it but leaves only. And he said to it: May no fruit ever come from you again." "And the fig withered at once."
Matthew 21:19—21

Bethany, General view

Bethany lies 2 miles east of Jerusalem on the eastern slope of the Mount of Olives and on the road to Jericho. This village, which since the 4th century carries the name of Lazarus (el Azarieh), was the home of Lazarus and his two sisters, Mary and Martha whom Jesus loved. He often visited them and their home was almost His home in Judea. Many happy events took place here. Here Christ taught the better way of life when he said to Martha, "Martha, Martha, you are anxious about too many things; only one is necessary; Mary has chosen the better part which shall not be taken from her." (Luke 10:38—42). Here Christ performed the great miracle of raising Lazarus from the dead. (John 11:1—44). Here, in the house of Simon the leper, Mary anointed Jesus with precious perfume. (Matthew 26:1—13, Mark 14:3—9, Luke 7:36—50, John 11:1—44).

Jesus said to her "I am the resurrection and the life, he who believes in me though he die, yet shall he live."
John 11:25

THE CHURCH OF LAZARUS

Two Byzantine churches were built over Lazarus' tomb. The first was destroyed by an earthquake and the second by the Persians in 614. In the 12th century, the Crusaders built a third church. After the fall of the Latin Kingdom, the shrines of Bethany were occupied by the Moslems. Only since the last century were the Franciscans able to buy the property. In 1949 they removed the old houses, excavated the site and discovered the remains of the previous churches and those of a Crusader monastery. Beautiful mosaic fragments from the 4th century church as well as buttresses of the Crusader church can be seen in the courtyard. The present church was built in 1952 on the foundations of the old churches.

Olive Oil Press

LAZARUS' TOMB

"It was a cave and a stone lay upon it." (John 11:38). It seems that the tomb of Lazarus was hewn in the rock within a cave. No wonder Jesus cried with a loud voice "Lazarus come forth." 22 steps lead down to a dark cave which is the traditional tomb of Lazarus. The original entrance, which must have been at ground level, was sealed by the Moslems who built a mosque between the church and the tomb. In the 17th century, the Franciscans obtained permission to make this new entrance which still leads down to the tomb.

EIN KAREM

"My soul magnifies the Lord and my spirit rejoices in God my Saviour."
Luke 1:46

The picturesque village Ein Karem, lying not far fro Jerusalem among hills su rounded by olive trees ar vineyards, is claimed to the birthplace of John th Baptist.

Here also Mary came fro Nazareth to visit her cous Elizabeth, the mother John. (Luke 1, 39—46) Th Gospel does not indicate th place where Mary me Elizabeth nor where Joh the Baptist was born. simply says that "Ma hastened into the hill count of Judah".

The site must have been hill country within eas reach of Jerusalem Zacharias was a priest serv ing in the Temple. Sever places were suggested f the site of the Visitation an the birth of John the Baptist. Tradition supported by archaeological and literary documents has fixed the site at Ein Karem. This charming village which corresponds to St. Luke's description with its spring of water must have attracted inhabitants since ancient times.

A church named after St. John the Baptist was built in the 5th century over the cave supposed to be part of the dwelling house of Zacharias and the site of the birth of John. It was destroyed, rebuilt by the Crusaders and again destroyed after their departure. The present church was built in 1885 by the Franciscan Fathers.

The two-storied church of the Visitation is built over the site where Elizabeth hid when she knew herself to be with child and where Mary came to visit her. The beginnings of this church go back to the 5th century. It was repeatedly restored and in 1938 the Franciscan Fathers built the Upper Church. On the wall facing the Church, the Magnificat is written in 41 languages on ceramic plaques.

Ein Karem, Church of the Visitation

Jericho lies in the Jordan valley, which is a great rift in the earth's crust, extending from Mount Hermon in the north to the gulf of Aqaba in the south, a distance of 280 miles. This rift continues through Kenya and Tanganyika to Mozambique. The lowest part of the depression is the region of the Dead Sea which is 1,300 feet below sea level, the lowest spot on earth. In the course of 25 miles, the land from Jerusalem (2,500 feet above sea level) falls 4,000 feet into the hot, sub-tropical world of the Jordan valley. The journey can lead to indisposition and temporary lack of hearing in view of the great difference in air pressure. Jericho, with its gardens, looks like a green carpet in the centre of that brown, sun-baked desert of the Jordan valley. Since very remote times, Jericho has been known for the richness of its well watered soil, its oranges, bananas and dates. In ancient times it was called the city of Palms. While in summer Jericho is very hot and airless, in winter and spring it has a wonderful climate with the odour of many different kinds of flowers. Jericho, with its rich soil, has been the cradle of civilization as far back as 7,000–10,000 B.C. It is considered the oldest city in the world to have been discovered so far. This stems from the result of archaeological excavations carried out in this century, mainly in 1952–56 by Miss Kathleen Kenyon. In the long course of time, the ruins of the towns which succeeded one another, have built up in

Jericho a "tell" or mound which is about 80 feet high and covers approximately ten acres. Dr. Sellin, an Austrian, was the first to start digging the tell of Jericho, known as Tell-el-Sultan, in 1908. In 1936, Garstang, of the British School of Archaeology, continued the works begun by Dr. Sellin and this was further continued by Miss Kathleen Kenyon in 1952–56. The result of the final excavations was the discovery of the earliest stratified levels ever found in any part of the world. Objects found were examined by the Carbon 14 method and dated to 7,000 B.C. On the rock bed, a very interesting neolithic tower was discovered. It is built of stones and mud with a pierced centre from top to bottom in which are twenty-two well built steps. It is dated to circa 7,000 B.C. In spite of its remote antiquity, Jericho entered history in the 13th century B.C. with the arrival of the Israelites into the Promised Land. It was the first city taken by the tribes of Israel after they crossed the river Jordan (Joshua 6). Joshua, after destroying and burning Jericho, cursed the man who should ever rebuild it. "And Joshua adjured them at that time saying 'Cursed be the man before the Lord, that riseth up and buildeth this city wall; on his eldest son he shall lay its foundations, on his youngest set up its gates.'" (Joshua 6:26). A few generations later, Jericho was rebuilt by Hiel the Bethelite, who was stricken with the curse of Joshua (I Kings 16:34). The prophet Elisha, at the urgent demands of the inhabitants, sweetened the water of one of its springs by casting into it a handful of salt (II Kings 2:19). This spring, which is the source of life of Jericho's green oasis, is located across the road from the ancient Jericho, and it carries the name of the prophet — Elisha's fountain. Jesus must have stopped in Jericho many times, certainly when he came to Jerusalem for the Passover, as Jericho was the meeting place for Jews coming from Galilee to Jerusalem at that time of the year. It was certainly in Jericho that Christ said to his disciples, "Now we are going up to Jerusalem and the Son of Man is about to be handed over to the chief priests and scribes; they will condemn Him to death and will hand Him over to the pagans to be mocked   d day He will rise again." (Matthew 20:   an (Luke 18:35–42) and it was here tha   tature climbed a sycamore tree so that he   come down, for this day I must abide ir

The Jericho hill.

THE MOUNT OF TEMPTATION

The Judean desert

The temptation of Jesus was immediately after His baptism in the Jordan river. "And Jesus being full of the Holy Ghost returned from Jordan and was led by the spirit into the wilderness." (Luke 4:1–13, Mark 1:12–13). Neither the Gospel nor any other source enables us to determine exactly the spot where Jesus underwent his forty days of fasting and temptations. Later tradition indicated the "Mount of Qarantal" which rises behind old Jericho, as the site of the first and third temptation. The summit of the mountain is indicated as the site of the last temptation, where the devil showed Him all the kingdoms of the world. At the slope of the eastern side of the mountain, a church was built in the 6th century over the cave designated to be the one occupied by Christ. This church was deserted in the 13th century and in 1874 the Greek Orthodox established themselves on the site and built a monastery.

THE RIVER JORDAN

Then Jesus came from Galilee to the Jordan to John to be baptized by him.
Matthew 3:13

This river is a strange stream which flows from the snow capped heights of Mount Hermon to the depths of the Dead Sea. It twists and curves in an 160 mile long bed, while the distance it covers is only 65 miles in a straight line. The Jordan Al Urdun (the Descender) deserves its name as it descends from 3,000 feet at Mount Hermon, where it is formed by the union of four streams, to the Dead Sea, 1,300 feet below sea level. Its average width is 100 feet. The Jordan river is holy to both the Old and the New Testaments. "John an austere looking figure clothed with camel's hair, eating locusts and honey, was preaching and baptizing along the lower reaches of the Jordan. Jesus came from Galilee to be baptised by John in the river Jordan. As soon as he was baptised he came up from the water, and suddenly the heavens opened and he saw the Spirit of God descending like a dove and coming down to him. And a voice spoke from heaven 'This is my beloved Son in whom I am well pleased.'" (Matthew 3, Mark 1, Luke 3). The traditional spot where Jesus was baptised is located some five miles east of Jericho. The baptism of Jesus in the Jordan made the river holy to all Christians who, since early times, went in a spirit of faith and piety to bathe in its waters. Thousands of pilgrims have come here to bathe in the Jordan, wearing white gowns which they take home to keep as their shrouds. Somewhere near the site of the Baptism, the Israelites, under Joshua, crossed the river and invaded the land. (Joshua 3:13–17). Somewhere near here, the prophet Elijah was taken by a chariot of fire into heaven. "There appeared a chariot of fire and Elijah went up by a whirlwind into heaven." (II Kings 2:11). Naaman was cured of leprosy by washing in the river Jordan. (II Kings 5:10–14).

Lot's Wife, salt pillar

Salt crystals and skeletons of trees covered with salt.

THE DEAD SEA

Bathing in the Dead Sea

The Dead Sea is 47 miles in length and 10 miles in width. It has a surface area of 360 square miles and its waters attain a maximum depth of 1,278 feet. It lies 1,300 feet below sea level, which is the lowest point on the earth's surface. It is called the Dead Sea because of the absence of any animal life in its waters. It is the most salt saturated water in the world, containing about 26 per cent solids. Ordinary water holds 4–6 per cent solids; thus the Dead Sea water contains five times more solids. The Dead Sea contains a huge concentration of chemicals since the Sea has no outlet. The River Jordan and other streams pour in tens of thousands of tons of water mixed with sulphurous and nitrous matter. This water unable to escape and subjected to the tremendous heat of the Jordan Valley evaporates, leaving behind a huge deposit of solid chemicals. The Dead Sea has unique healing properties owing to the high mineral content of its water. Research shows that the water contains thousands of millions of metric tons of calcium chloride, magnesium, sodium and potassium. Its specific gravity is 1.166 which keeps the body from sinking and one can thus relax on the water without making the slightest movement.

The caves

QUMRAN

In 1947 a Bedouin looking for a stray goat, in the western region of the Dead Sea area, made the greatest find of this century by discovering the now famous Dead Sea Scrolls. An Arab shepherd named Mohammed Edib, looking for a lost goat, threw a stone into the opening of a cave and heard the clatter of something breaking. He ran away afraid thinking that the cave was inhabited by spirits. However, on the next day he called his cousin and both entered the cave and found eight jars, some with their lids still on; they took the jars outside and started searching in the hope of finding gold inside them. They were disappointed when they only found bundles of leather with columns of writing of which they were unable to understand the slightest thing. A total of seven scrolls were found. One day the Bedouin brought his strange find to a Syrian Christian named Khalil Kando and sold them to him. Kando took four of the scrolls he had bought and showed them to his Metropolitan who resided in Jerusalem. The Metropolitan recognised the four scrolls as ancient Hebrew writing and immediately bought them. In 1949, after realising that the scrolls were of great value, he took them to the United States where they were bought by Professor Yigael Yadin for $250,000 and then brought to Israel. Professor Eleazar Sukenik, Yadin's father, had already purchased the other three scrolls from Bethlehem. The scrolls are now exhibited in the museum of the Shrine of the Book in Jerusalem. The most famous scroll is the one of Isaiah which is one foot wide by 24 feet long. In 1949, Professor Harding, director of antiquities in Jordan, Père de Vaux, director of the Ecole Biblique and the Bedouins, aware of the high price of the scrolls, started searching all over the western region of the Dead Sea. More than 900 pieces of scrolls were found in more than 30 caves. The largest quantity of manuscripts came from cave IV, discovered by the Bedouin in 1952 and only 100 yards from the ruins of

Steps leading to the cistern

Qumran. The scrolls were written on leather and papyrus, apart from two, which were written on copper. According to Josephus and Pliny, the writers of the Dead Sea scrolls had been identified as the Essenes. The Essenes were members of a religious sect who, detesting the life of corruption, retired to the hot desert on the shores of the Dead Sea. They abandoned Jerusalem for an austere desert, leading a life of prayer, study, meditation, poverty and charity. Members had to surrender all their properties to the Order as they lived a perfect communal life. Josephus wrote that they were "Communists to perfection." The Essenes settled Qumran about the first century B.C. In the year 31 B.C. they abandoned their settlement which was destroyed by an earthquake. Thirty years later the same sect returned, repaired their small village and resettled it. By 68 B.C. the Essenes had all been massacred by Titus' soldiers who were on their way to crush the Jewish revolt in Jerusalem. At the approach of the Roman legions, the Essenes hurriedly hid their most valuable possessions, their Scriptures, in the caves around their settlement and in inaccessible caves high up the side of the nearby cliffs. The desert kept their secret for 2,000 years until their accidental discovery in 1947.

The Habakkuk Commentary, one of the seven Dead Sea Scrolls housed in the "Shrine of the Book" in Jerusalem

THE RUINS OF QUMRAN

The private living quarters of the sect were huts, tents and caves near the community centre. The centre of the community was found and completely excavated in 1951–56. The ruins comprise a main building 120 feet long by 90 feet wide, constructed of large roughly dressed stones. On the north side, stood a defence tower which was three storeys high. One long, narrow room served as a dining room in which a pile of ceramic dishes was found. Over a thousand ceramic bowls were found in an adjoining room which was probably the kitchen. The most interesting find was the scriptorium with its benches and writing tables. Two inkstands, one of bronze and another of clay were discovered with dried ink in the former. The compound around the main building comprised a dyer's shop, stable, pottery workshop, mill and seven cisterns. These cisterns were filled with rain water channelled from the mountains by an aqueduct, the remains of which can still be seen. East of the settlement lies the cemetery containing some 1100 graves.

MASSADA

About $2\frac{1}{2}$ miles from the western shore of the Dead Sea, in the wilderness of Judah, stands the rock fortress of Massada. It is $\frac{1}{2}$ mile long, 220 yards wide and rises 2,000 feet above the level of the Dead Sea. It is cut out of the mountain range by deep gorges which surround its base. Alexander Jannai, the High Priest, was the first to build a fortress on the summit of Massada in the middle of the second century B.C. In the year 40 B.C. Herod the Great built a huge, magnificent fortress on the top of Massada, and, by his own account, "fortified it to protect himself from the Jews should they try and depose him." He embellished it for use as a residence in case he was removed from his kingdom by Mark Anthony. The fortress had been strongly fortified by an 18 foot high wall with 38 towers, each 75 feet high. Inside there were store houses, barracks, arsenals, large cisterns filled by rain water and all kinds of royal accommodation. It was a master-piece of engineering. Massada has become a shrine for the Jews, as it is the site of one of the most dramatic episodes in their history. It is the symbol of courage and heroism and of the choice of death over slavery. In the year 70 A.D. when the Roman legions subdued the whole of Palestine and Jerusalem was beaten into the dust, a band of Jewish patriots, led by Eleazar Ben Yair, marched on Massada, overwhelmed the Roman garrison and captured it. Joined later by a few surviving patriots who evaded capture in Jerusalem, they were determined to continue their fight against the Romans and made Massada a base for their guerilla strikes. In the year 72, Silva, one of Titus' generals, decided to destroy this outpost at all cost. He marched on that great rock with his best soldiers, the 10th legion, auxiliary troops and thousands of prisoners carrying water and provisions. Silva prepared himself for a long siege and built a wall 3 miles in circumference around the fortress. At strategic points around the base, he established eight military camps whose remains can still be distinguished. The blockade was complete and the besieged were cut off from the rest of the country. For many months the Romans tried to storm the fortress but were beaten back as it was well fortified and defended. Then they built a ramp, and moved a battering ram up the ramp directing it against the fortress wall until they finally made a breach. It was the beginning of the end. The defenders built an inner wall of earth encased in wood but the Romans set it on fire by using firebrands. Their leader, Eleazar Ben Yair, knew that the Romans would overrun them finally the following morning. He gathered his men around him and delivered one of the most dramatic speeches in history. "Life is the calamity for men, not death. All men are equally destined to death, and the same fate attends the coward as the brave. Can we think of submitting to the indignity of slavery? Can we behold our wives dishonoured and our children enslaved? While freedom is our own and we are in possession of our swords, let us make a determined use of them to preserve our liberties. Let us die free men, gloriously surrounded by our wives and children. And let us be expeditious. Eternal renown shall be ours by snatching the prize from the hands of our enemies and leaving them nothing to triumph over but the bodies of those who dared to be their own executioners." This is how Josephus describes the heroic and dramatic end of 960 people who decided to die by their own hand rather than surrender to their enemies. "While they embraced their wives and children for the last time, they wept over and stabbed them in the same moment, taking comfort, however, that this work was not to be performed by their enemies... There was not one man who was wanting in the necessary courage... They then cast lots for the selection of ten men out of their number to destroy the rest. These being chosen,

Herod's Palace

the devoted victims embraced the bodies of their deceased families and then ranging themselves near them, resigned themselves to the hands of the executioners. When these ten had discharged their disagreable task, they again cast lots as to which of the ten should kill the other nine. The nine devoted victims died with the same resolution as their brethren had done. The surviving man, having surveyed the bodies and found that they were all dead, set fire to the palace and threw himself on his sword among his companions." At dawn the next day, the Romans attacking the fortress were astonished at the lack of opposition. On entering the fortress they saw the bodies and heard the story from two women who had hidden themselves with five children. Josephus wrote — "Far, however, from exulting in the triumph of joy that might have been expected from enemies, they united to admire the steady virtue and dignity of mind with which the Jews had been inspired, and wondered at their contempt of death by which such numbers had been bound in one solemn pact. For the Romans it was a hollow victory." Excavations of Massada started only in 1955–56 when Professor Yigael Yadin, with volunteers from many countries, excavated the entire summit of Massada. Very important and interesting remains have been found and some of the writings of Josephus, thought by many scholars to be legendary, were confirmed.

Samaritan women

Then came a woman of Samaria, to draw water. Jesus said to her "Give me a drink."

John 4:7

JACOB'S WELL

Everyone who drinks of this water will thirst again, but whoever drinks of the water that I shall give him, will never thirst...

John 4:13—14

Jacob, on his return from Mesopotamia, came to the valley lying between the two mountains Gerizim and Ebal, as did Abraham before him. He bought a piece of land on which he pitched his tent and dug a well for himself, his children and his flocks. Since that time, the well has been known as Jacob's well. It was at this same well that Christ met the Samaritan woman and asked her for water to drink (John 4). St. John mentioned that this sublime dialogue took place at Jacob's well. The Old Jewish and Christian traditions, affirm that this is the authentic well dug by Jacob, and at which Christ talked to the Samaritan woman. The well is $7\frac{1}{2}$ feet in diameter, 90 feet deep and contains soft water. In the fourth century, a church was built here with the well in the centre of its crypt. The church was damaged during the Samaritan revolt in 529 and restored under the Emperor Justinian. The church was again destroyed and rebuilt by the Crusaders. In 1187, the church was destroyed by Saladin. It was only in 1860 that the Greeks took possession of the ruins and restored the crypt. The work begun on a new church in 1914 was suspended and has not been resumed.

THE SAMARITANS

numbering 400 people (240 in Nablus and 160 in Holon) are the strangest and most ancient sect in the world. They have remained pure in blood for 2,500 years. The separation between the Samaritans and the Jews began after the return from the Babylonian captivity. The Jews refused to consider the inhabitants of Samaria, who escaped deportation, as Jews, because they had mingled with the colonist Assyrians. They also refused to allow them to share in the rebuilding of the Temple. The

Samaritans, with implacable hatred, separated themselves from the Jews and built a rival temple on Mount Gerizim. From the Bible, they only recognise the five books of Moses and their most interesting possession is an ancient copy of the Pentateuch written on parchment. They claim that their Pentateuch is the oldest hand written book in the world and that it was written by Aaron, Moses' brother, 3,600 years ago. Scholars date their book to the 12th century A.D. Many of the Samaritans are poor and some are mentally sick as they only marry within their own group. Each year at Passover time, they sacrifice lambs on the top of their holy mountain, Gerizim.

NAZARETH

And the Word was made flesh, and dwelt among us.
John 1:14

One of the main Christian holy cities of The Holy Land, stands at a height of 1,230 feet above sea level. This city, enshrined amongst hills, was the place chosen by God for the annunciation of the birth of His Son, and where He grew to manhood. (Luke 1:26–35). Here "the word became flesh and dwelt among us." (John 1:14). Here Jesus spent his childhood playing in the streets and on the hills with nothing to distinguish him from the other children of Nazareth. Here he spent his hidden thirty years working probably as a carpenter with Joseph. St. Luke calls him "The Carpenter." The streets of Nazareth which must have looked like the narrow present ones, its hills which are the same, had been the scene of the life of Jesus for thirty years. At the time of Jesus, it seems that Nazareth as a little town, had a bad reputation, which made Nathanael from the neighbouring village of Cana, hearing people talk of Jesus of Nazareth, exclaim: "Can anything good come out of Nazareth?" Jesus himself was not understood in his home city. "Amen I say to you that no prophet is accepted in his own country." (Luke 4:24). The first attempt on Jesus' life was made in Nazareth. Hearing his criticism and his speaking as a teacher of authority "They were filled with wrath, rose up and thrust him out of the city, and led him into the brow of the hill whereon their city was built, that they might cast him down headlong." (Luke 4:28–29). The hill has long been identified as the Mount of Precipitation. After this attempt, Jesus abandoned Nazareth and went down to Capernaum, which became his city. There is no definite date when Nazareth came into being. The spring, which still supplies the well

(Mary's well) with water, must have attracted inhabitants since very ancient times. At the time of Jesus, Nazareth was larger than a village and was always called a city. Nazareth did not have any dramatic history. In 66 A.D. the city was destroyed by Vespasian, and, after the defeat of the Bar Kokhba revolt, it was inhabited by the many Jews who fled to Galilee. In 629 the Jews were expelled from Nazareth by Heraclius as they had joined the Persians in 614 to fight against the Christians. During the Crusader period, the city revived and prospered. Tancred, "Prince of Galilee" rebuilt the city churches and monasteries. In 1187 the city was taken by Saladin; in 1263 it was destroyed by Bibars and after that the city remained Moslem for 400 years. In 1620 Christian families began settling here. The town grew little by little and today Nazareth houses the largest Arab community in Israel (35,000) the majority being Christians.

Nazareth, inhabited by Jews after the great Jewish revolt, became accessible to Christians only in the 4th century. In the beginning of the 5th century, a church was built over the grotto of the Annunciation, and was probably destroyed in 614 by the Persians. Tancred rebuilt the monastery and the church in Roman style, In 1263, the Crusader church was razed to the ground by Bibars. In 1730 the Franciscans were permitted to build a small church which they enlarged in 1877. The Franciscans had always wanted to erect a church worthy of the great mystery of the Annunciation, and their dream was realised in 1960–68. They built a magnificent church, which is one of the largest Christian sanctuaries in the Middle East. Before the Franciscans built their church, they excavated the entire area. Remains of the previous buildings were discovered. Among the discoveries, a base of a column from the Byzantine church was found with the invocation of "EX MARIA", Greek for "Hail Mary."

Market scene

THE CHURCH OF THE ANNUNCIATION

This magnificent church was designed by the Italian architect Muzio, who achieved great architectural renown. He conceived a plan of two interconnected churches, one above the other, preserving in full the remains of the ancient churches. The outer walls of the lower church followed the lines of the Crusaders' Basilica, except that they were moved a few yards from the west to separate the building from the busy main road. The two churches are 80 feet high and 130 feet long. The western and southern facades are decorated with statues illustrating the Incarnation and the Annunciation. The striking majestic dome is 170 feet high and is made of reinforced concrete with stone. Its roof is covered with copper and the cupola is surmounted by a lantern.

THE GROTTO OF THE ANNUNCIATION

The grotto is situated at what was the extreme southern end of the ancient village. This grotto is believed to be the traditional site of the Annunciation.

MARY'S WELL

is one of the most authentic sites in the Holy Land. It was and still is the city's only water supply. There is no doubt that Jesus, with his mother, came here to draw water as the women and children of Nazareth have always done. The spring gushes out of the mountain and runs through a conduit to a public fountain where women still draw water all day long. The Greek Orthodox claim that the Annunciation took place while the Virgin Mary was drawing water from the fountain over which they eventually built their own church.

CANA

The Water Jug

There are three or four places of that name which claim to be the Cana of the New Testament; Cana, which lies 4 miles along the road from Nazareth to Tiberias, is the most favoured one. Cana is known throughout the entire Christian world, as it was the scene of Jesus' first miracle when "he changed water into wine" (John 2:1–11). Two churches are built in Cana commemorating this first miracle.

THE HORNS OF HITTIN

are so called because of their shape, the two tops resembling 'horns'. The Horns of Hittin became famous as the site where Saladin defeated the Crusaders in 1187 and brought to an end their eighty year old Latin Kingdom of Jerusalem. In that battle, 20,000 Christians were killed and 30,000 were taken prisoner with their king, Guy of Lusignan. The wood of the true cross was taken and sent to Damascus. After that battle, Crusader strongholds surrendered one after the other without difficulty.

TIBERIAS

lies 682 feet below sea level on the west side of the Sea of Galilee. This city was founded in the year 26 A.D. by Herod Antipas and named Tiberias in honour of the Roman Emperor Tiberius. Herod built the city with beautiful palaces, theatres, temples shining with gold and marble, and public baths over the hot springs, which were famous throughout the Roman world for their healing properties. Tiberias also had the advantage of being situated at one of the most beautiful sites in the world, a site which was described by Josephus as "the ambition of nature." While Tiberias is not Biblical, it is a holy Jewish city. After the Bar Kokhba revolt, Hadrian decreed the expulsion of all Jews from Jerusalem. Tiberias replaced Jerusalem and became the dwelling place of the great sages and the religious and intellectual Jewish centre. In Tiberias, the Mishna was compiled in about the year 200 A.D. The Talmudic school produced the Jerusalem Talmud at the end of the 4th century. Vowels and punctuation were introduced into the Hebrew language. Many Jewish sages are buried in Tiberias. The most famous is Rabbi Maimonides, the great philosopher of his time and physician at the court of Saladin in Cairo. He spent most of his life in Cairo and died there in 1204 but his remains were brought and buried in Tiberias. Rabbi Meir who lived in the 2nd century, is buried here and is much venerated by Orthodox Jews and credited with the working of miracles. Other rabbis buried here include Rabbi Yohanan ben Zakkai, Rabbi Akiva, Rabbis Ami and Assi and Rabbi Horovitz.

Tomb of Rabbi Meir Baal Haness

In 637, Tiberias was occupied by the Moslems. In 1099 it was captured by the crusaders and became the capital of Galilee. After the famous battle of Hittin, it surrendered to the Moslems. In the 16th century, under Turkish rule, Tiberias had been made a semi-independent Jewish town under the rule of the Jewish Don Yossef Nassi. In 1837 the entire city was completely destroyed by an earthquake. At present all the inhabitants of Tiberias are Jewish, and many of them are new-comers. It is the most popular winter resort in Israel.

THE SEA OF GALILEE

It was on the slopes of this beautiful lake-side, that Jesus began to preach the Kingdom of God.

is 13 miles long, 7 miles wide, 130—157 feet deep, 32 miles in circumference and 686 feet below sea level. The lake has been known by various names — Sea of Galilee, Tiberias, and Kinneret which comes from the Hebrew word for harp, as the sea is shaped like a harp. The sea is abundant in fish — carp, mullet, sardine, catfish and combfish. As in ancient times, the fish are still caught in nets. The water is pure and generally calm. At the time of Jesus, Galilee was the centre of roads crossing in all directions. The good communications, the extreme fertility of the valley, the beauty of the landscape and the hot springs of Tiberias, drew a considerable population, and the whole area was a scene of continuous activity. The sea of Galilee, as a central feature, was surrounded by nine cities. George Adam Smith in 1894 describes the lake thus: "Sweet water, full of fish, a surface of sparkling blue. The lake of Galilee is at once food, drink and air, a rest to the eye, coolness in the heat, an escape from the crowd." Smith goes on, "Where there are now no trees, there were great woods, where there are marshes, there were noble gardens, where there is but one boat, there were fleets of sail." Father Eugene Hoade describes the lake — "I believe that there are beautiful lakes in the world, set in more enchanting surroundings, but I still believe that there is not in the world a more fascinating lake. Look at its azure blue in deep sleep without a ripple on its bosom, the little sailing boats as if just painted on the canvas, not a breath of air to disturb in its waters the great reflections of the surrounding mountains; it is a joy that leads on to hourless contemplation." It was on the slopes of this beautiful lake-side described as the "ambition of nature", in this valley full of activity, that Jesus began to preach the Kingdom of God. Here Jesus spent most of his public life, gave most of his teachings and worked most of his miracles. On the sea shore, Jesus called Peter, Andrew, James and other apostles (Matthew 4:18—20, Luke 5:1—11); healed a leper (Matthew 8:1—4); spoke to the multitudes from Peter's boat (Mark 3:7—12, Luke 5:1—3); commanded the violent storm to be still (Matthew 8:23—27); walked on the stormy water (Matthew 14:22—23) and healed great multitudes (Matthew 15:29—31). The twelve apostles were ordained on a mountain near the sea. (Mark 3:13—19).

MAGDALA

The "Tower of Greatness" is locat[ed] 4 miles north of Tiberias. Today it i[s] small village of fishermen. At the ti[me] of Christ it was a city of considera[ble] importance. According to Josephus had 40,000 inhabitants and a fleet 230 boats. Josephus fortified the c[ity] before he deserted to the Roma[ns.] When the city fell to Titus, 6,700 Je[ws] were killed, 6,000 of the strongest w[ere] sent to Nero to dig the Corinth Ca[nal] and 30,000 were auctioned off slaves. Magdala became famous as it[s] the birth place of Mary Magdalene, t[he] woman Jesus healed from evil spir[its] and infirmities (Luke 8:2). Mary Ma[g]dalene then became one of the m[ost] devoted and faithful of Christ's f[ol]lowers. She followed Him to His dea[th] on Calvary. She was the first to co[me] to the tomb on the day of His resu[r]rection and the first to see the Ris[en] Lord (John 20:1−14).

"Follow me and I will make you become fishers of men. And immediately they left their nets and followed Him."
Mark 1:17−18

Tabgha, the Church of St. Peter's Primacy

St. Peter's fishes

Mosaic of the loaves and fishes

TABGHA

"We have only five loaves here and two fish."
Matthew 14:17

This name comes from the Greek word Heptapegon meaning seven springs. It is a place with a plentiful supply of water. Traditionally this is the site where Jesus fed 5000 with 5 loaves and two fish (Mark 6:36–44, Matthew 14:13–21, John 6:1–6). Two successive Byzantine churches were built here in the 4th and 5th centuries. In 1932, the remains of a Byzantine church were discovered with the best preserved mosaic in all Israel. On the stone which served as the altar, there is a mosaic of a basket of loaves flanked by two fish. The floor is covered with a beautiful mosaic of birds, fish, beasts and flowers of the lake region. In 1934, a new church was built over the site of the Byzantine church. Two hundred yards away, is the church of the Primacy, built in 1934 in basalt over a massive rock called the "Mensa Christ." It is the traditional site where the Risen Lord appeared to His disciples, prepared breakfast for them and gave Peter the pastoral commission of "Feed my sheep." (John 21:9).

CAPERNAUM

*"And they went into
Capernaum, and
immediately on the
Sabbath he entered
The Synagogue
and taught."*

Mark 1:21

is located 2½ miles from where the Jordan enters the Sea of Galilee. It was a customs station on the way to Damascus and the residence of a high Roman officer. It was a busy city, where merchants used to bring the silk and spices from Damascus, and take back the dried fish, and the fruits of the plains of Gennessaret. As Jesus was not understood in Nazareth, and the first attempt on his life was made there, he turned his back on his city, went to Capernaum and made it his second native city. Capernaum then became the centre of his activities for about 20 months. Here He pronounced many of his speeches and manifested his goodness and omnipotence by many miracles. Capernaum was the home of St. Peter. Jesus taught here in the synagogue (Mark 1:21, Luke 4:31–33); delivered here a man of unclean spirit and healed Peter's mother-in-law (Matthew 8:14–17, Mark 1:21–34, Luke 4:31–41). Here Jesus healed the centurion's servant (Matthew 8:5–13, Luke

7:1–10); and the palsied man when he was let down through the roof (Matthew 9:1–8, Mark 2:1–12, Luke 5:17–20). Here too Jesus raised Jarius' daughter from the dead (Matthew 9:18–26, Mark 5:22–43, Luke 8:41–56); healed the woman who had an issue of blood (Matthew 9:20–22, Mark 5:25–35, Luke 8:43–48); healed two blind men (Matthew 9:27–35); healed the son of a nobleman (John 4:46–54); healed the withered hand (Matthew 12:10–14, Mark 3:1–6, Luke 6:6–11) and healed great multitudes brought to him (Matthew 8:16–17; 9:36–38). Jesus pronounced a curse on the city thus: "And thou, Capernaum, which art exalted into heaven, shall be brought down to hell, for if the mighty works which have been done in thee, had been done in Sodom, it would have remained until this day. But I say to you, that it shall be more tolerable for the land of Sodom in the day of judgement, than for thee." (Matthew 11:23–24). The prophecy of Jesus about the ungrateful city of Capernaum was fulfilled; the site of the city was uncertain for a long time. Today, Capernaum is no more than a heap of rubble beside the lake shore. In 1905, two German archaeologists began exploring the site and their work, was completed in 1926 by the Franciscan fathers. The most important find was the discovery of the now famous Capernaum synagogue. This synagogue was built in the 3rd century over the ruins of a synagogue built by the centurion whose servant was healed by Jesus (Luke 7). Jewish and Roman symbols are carved on the stones. Among the Jewish symbols are the Shofar, the star of David, the Menorah, the Ark of the Covenant and the palm, which is the old Jewish symbol of the land. It is very probable that some of the carved stones of the first synagogue were incorporated in the decoration of the second. Christians venerate the synagogue at Capernaum where Jesus worshipped, taught and wrought miracles. Some of the stones still standing, once echoed with his voice and witnessed his miracles. The Franciscans continued the excavations and exposed what is believed to be the house of St. Peter with the remains of a 5th century church above it.

"Whoever receive one such child in my name receives me, but whoever causes one of these little ones who believe in me to sin, it would be better for him to have a great millstone fastened, round his neck, and to be drowned into the depth of the sea."

Matthew 18:5–6

Relief of the Holy Ark

*"Blessed are the p
in spirit for theirs i.
the Kingdom of
heaven. Blessed ar
the peacemakers, ﬁ
they shall be callee
sons of God.*

Matthew !

THE MOUNT OF THE BEATITUDES

is the traditional site where Jesus uttered the immortal words of
the beatitudes and the most wonderful principles of the blessed life.
"Blessed are the poor in spirits for theirs is the kingdom of Heaven..."
(Matthew 5). In 1937, the Franciscans built a church over the
mount with a superb view of the lake — "The Church of the
Beatitudes."

*Simon Peter replied
"You are the Christ,
the Son of the living
God."*

Matthew 16:16

CAESAREA PHILIPI (BANIAS)

In his travels, Jesus reached as far north as Caesarea Philipi. Its present name Banias, is a corruption of the Greek word Paneas, for here stood a shrine to the god Pan. Built by Herod the Great, the city was embellished and named Caesarea, by his son Philip. It was here that Simon Pelei acknowledged Jesus as the Messiah "You are the Christ the son of the living God". Mathew 16:16.

Jordan River and Mt. Hermon

*"Consider the lilies,
how they grow, they
neither toil nor spin,
yet I tell you, even
Solomon in all his
glory was not arrayed
like one of these."*

Luke 12:27

The Lily of the Fields   89

MOUNT TABOR

Mt. Tabor rises abruptly 1,600 feet above the surrounding plain and 1,900 feet above sea level. It is the most picturesque and striking mountain in Galilee. In Psalm 89, David sings that "Tabor and Hermon shall rejoice in the name of the Lord." To the psalmist, its strength and beauty are a testimony to the Creator. In ancient times it was a frontier line between the northern and southern tribes. It was considered a holy mount for Israel, as it was a witness to the glory of God manifested in the important victory of Barak, fore-told by the prophetess Deborah, over the strong Canaanite army of Sisera (Judges 4:6). The Arab village at the foot of the mountain is named "Daburieh" in honour of the prophetess Deborah. For the Christians, Mount Tabor is a holy place as it was chosen by Jesus to be the site of His Transfiguration (Luke 9:28–36). The summit of Mount Tabor, 1,300 yards long and 450 yards wide, is surrounded by the remains of a fortress wall built in the 13th century by the Moslems. In 1924, the Franciscans built a church here — the Church of the Transfiguration — incorporating the new construction with the remains of previous churches. Besides the remains of the older Byzantine church of the 6th century and the 12th century Crusader church, are ruins of ancient strongholds and monasteries. From the summit there is a splendid view of almost the entire region.

"Tabor and Hermon shall rejoice in the name of the Lord."
Psalms 89:13

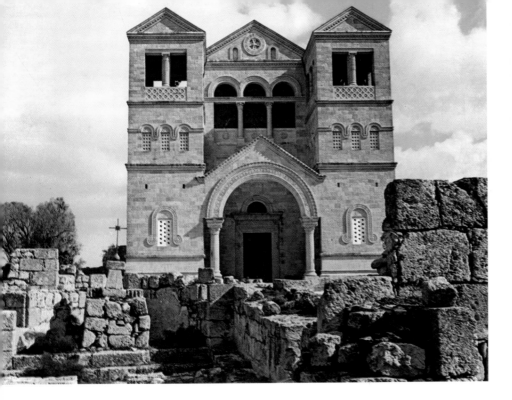

The Church of the Transfiguration, Mt. Tabor

stretches between the mountains of Galilee in the north and the mountains of Samaria in the south. It is the largest valley in Israel. It has the shape of a triangle, 15 by 15 by 20 miles. It was famous in ancient times, as today, for its fertility. It is known as the "Breadbasket of Israel." The strategic position and fertility of this plain made it one of the most famous battlefields of the ancient world. More than 20 battles have been fought for its control. Hebrews, Canaanites, Midianites, Syrians, Egyptians, Assyrians, Babylonians, Greeks, Romans, Arabs, Crusaders, Turks and lastly the British under Allenby during the First World War, fought on its soil.

THE VALLEY OF JEZREEL

View of the Jezreel valley

The water system

MEGIDDO

is located on the southern edge of the plain of Jezreel, where the Way of the Sea (Via Maris) leaves the plain and passes through a long and narrow defile into the plain of Sharon by the coast. Megiddo is the strategic point at the opening of this defile, which was the great highway connecting the land of Egypt and the south, with Syria and the north. Peoples stretching to the fertile coast of the Mediterranean, and the western conquerors invading the north and east, had to pass through this defile, fighting their way past Megiddo, which stands at its most strategic position. Around its gates and ruins have fought Egyptians, Canaanites, Philistines, Israelites, Assyrians, Greeks, Romans, Persians and the British in the 1st world war. The strategic position of Megiddo was recognised by Allenby, who, in 1917, made it the base of his campaign against the Turks. The numerous battles fought at Megiddo made it a symbol of war. Christian tradition envisions that the last and final great battle of the world shall be fought at Megiddo. "They go forth unto the kings of the earth and of the whole to gather them to the battle of the great day of God Almighty; and he gathered them together into a place called in the Hebrew tongue Armageddon." (Mount of Megiddo); (Rev. 16.16). Megiddo was first mentioned in ancient Egyptian writings. In 1478 B.C. King Thutmose of Egypt waged war upon the city, and the plans of his battle were written on the walls of his temple in upper Egypt. Joshua captured the city and killed the king (Joshua 12:21). In the 10th century B.C. Solomon rebuilt and fortified the city, financing its construction with a special levy. It became one of his cities of chariots and

Model of the City in King Solomon's time.

bulwark for the defence of his kingdom. Ahaziah, King of Judah, was killed here by Jehu (II Kings 23:29–30). Josiah, the good and great king, was killed here while attempting to prevent Pharoah Necho of Egypt from marching on the Euphrates. "His servants carried him in a chariot dead from Megiddo and brought him to Jerusalem and buried him in his own town (II Kings 23:30). The mount of Megiddo was excavated between 1925 and 1939 by the Oriental Institute of the University of Chicago. Excavations covering an area of 13 acres revealed the remains of 20 superimposed cities, each one being represented by a distinct layer of ruins. Among the very important discoveries are Solomon's stables capable of housing 450 horses and 150 chariots; grain silos, remains of walls, houses and foundations of gates of different periods. An exquisite collection of ivories, one of the finest of its kind in the world was also found. An ingenious water system supplied the city with fresh water from a spring outside the city wall. A shaft was dug into the ground to a depth of 120 feet, a tunnel 215 feet long was cut in the rock connecting the shaft with the spring outside the city, and the opening of the spring was covered with earth to hide it from invaders.

"And he gathered them together into a place called in the Hebrew tongue Armageddon."
Rev. 16:16

Eastern Gate

Pillar and manger in stable

ACRE

one of the oldest cities in the world was first mentioned in the Scriptures under the name of AKKO as the town of the tribe of Asher (Judges 1:31). It was a Canaanite and then a Phoenician port that commanded the approach to the plain of Jezreel from the sea. In the 3rd century B.C., the Greeks changed its name to Ptolemais and this was the name of the city when it was visited by St. Paul on his way to Jerusalem (Acts 21:7). Acre, during its long history, has been occupied by different people but the great history of this city began with the Crusaders. In 1104, Baldwin the First conquered the city to secure the sea ports. He fortified it and it became one of the main bulwarks of the Latin Kingdom in Palestine. Acre revived, prospered and became the landing sea port of all Europeans coming to the Holy Land either to visit and pray or to fight. After the battle of Hittin, the city surrendered to Saladin. Two years later, the Christians attacked the city and after great battles, the city capitulated. The Crusaders, unable to reconquer Jerusalem, made Acre the capital of their kingdom. Acre then enjoyed great prosperity for a hundred years until its fall in 1291. Sultan Al Ashraf besieged Acre with 200,000 soldiers. The city fell and the army of the Sultan devestated the city by fire and killed almost everybody without mercy. The fall of Acre in 1291 was the end of the Crusaders' Kingdom of Palestine which lasted for 200 years (1099–1291). Acre was destroyed to prevent any western power from regaining a foothold in the country. In 1775, Acre was rebuilt and fortified by an Albanian soldier Ahmed Al Jazzar, known as the "Butcher" on account of his cruelty. In 1799 Napoleon besieged Acre which was defended by Al Jazzar and the British fleet under

Sir Sidney Smith. In spite of all efforts, Napoleon failed to conquer the city and retreated to Egypt ending his dream of an eastern empire. In 1832, Ibrahim Pasha of Egypt took it from the Turks and kept it for only eight years, as he was forced to withdraw when the city was bombarded by the fleets of the European allies of Turkey. After that, Acre gradually declined and was at last overshadowed by the neighbouring city of Haifa. Today, Acre is inhabited by Jews, mainly newcomers, with small communities of Moslems and Christians. Crusader and Turkish ruins are the only remains of the long, stirring history of Acre which has had 17 recorded sieges. The most important remains of the Crusader period is the crypt of St. John which is believed to be the dining hall of the Knights Hospitallers of St. John. From the time of the Turks there remains the citadel, a rampart built to guard the city from coastal attack. Another important Turkish remain is the mosque built by Al Jazzar. It is considered to be the largest and most splendid mosque in Israel, and is built over the ruins of a Crusader cathedral. Near the Mosque is a twin domed building housing the tombs of Ahmed Al Jazzar, builder of the mosque, and his successor Suleiman Pasha.

The Mansion of Baha'i

HAIFA

Haifa, a small town of 10,000 at the beginning of this century, is now the third largest city in Israel, with a population of about 225,000. It possesses the country's main port and the nation's largest heavy industries. It is, at the same time, situated in the most beautiful bay of the Mediterranean coast, and on the slopes of the most charming mountain in Israel — Mount Carmel. The origin of Haifa is obscure. Its name appears for the first time only in the 3rd century A.D. in Talmudic literature. It is not associated with any major military or historical

Bahai Archives building

event. Haifa, as a small town, was occupied in turn by the Crusaders, the Arabs, the Turks and the British. In 1898, Theodor Herzl, founder of Zionism, visited Haifa and prophesied a future, larger city. His praise attracted thousands of early immigrants and Haifa is today, one of the most important cities in Israel. One of the main features of Haifa is that it is the world centre of the Bahai faith of some 2,000,000 followers.

The Bahai faith, began in Persia in 1844. Its leaders were exiled to Acre. They believe in the brotherhood of all men, unity of all religions, a common world language and that all prophets were sent by God to preach the same message, the most recent being Baha Ullah (founder of their faith). They have a very beautiful shrine in Haifa, which is considered their holy city.

Mt. Carmel and River Kishon

MOUNT CARMEL

is 16 miles long by 4–5 miles wide and 1,800 feet high. Its name is derived from the Hebrew "Karem El" which means vineyards of God. In ancient times it was covered by vineyards and was at all times famous for its fertility. It remains green throughout the year and is the most charming mountain in Israel. It had been a symbol of beauty and grace for the prophets and its heights served as altars for different gods since ancient times. Mount Carmel was forever renowned as being the scene of contest between monotheism and paganism, as it was here that the prophet Elijah challenged the priests of Baal and confounded them when their incantations failed and his own drew fire from heaven (Kings 18). At the foot of Mount Carmel, near the coastal suburb, is the sacred cave of the prophet Elijah. It is believed that here Elijah took refuge during one of his flights from the anger of King Ahab (I Kings 19:8–13). The cave is a sacred Jewish shrine, venerated also by Christians and Moslems who revere Elijah as the hero of the triumph of monotheism. The Carmelite monastic order established themselves here in the 13th century with the prophet Elijah as their patron saint.

The river of Kishon swept them away, that ancient river, the river Kishon

Judges 21:5

CAESAREA

In the year 20 B.C. Herod the Great rebuilt the town of Caesarea along the Mediterranean coast, begun as a small Phoenician town under the name of "Strato's Tower." The most skilled architects and engineers of that time spent twelve years working and when they finished, had constructed one of the most beautiful cities of Palestine and one of the most striking port cities of that period. The city was beautified with splendid palaces, public buildings, market place, magnificent marble temple, amphitheatre and hippodrome. He also built an ingenious artificial harbour in which great ships could safely lie at anchor. Massive stones were lowered into the sea to form a semi-circular jetty 200 feet wide. Herod named the city Caesarea in honour of his master, Augustus Caesar. After Herod's death, Caesarea passed under Roman rule, and because of its beauty, it was chosen to be the seat of the Roman procurators. Pontius Pilate lived in Caesarea and from here he went to Jerusalem for the Passover during which time he condemned Jesus to the cross. A stone bearing his name was discovered here. Caesarea then served as the capital of the Roman government of Palestine for about 500 years. Philip the Deacon lived and evangelised here (Acts 8:40). Here St. Peter preached to Cornelius who became the first gentile convert (Acts 21:8). Here St. Paul was imprisoned for two years and here he testified to the Risen Lord before Agrippa and all the notables (Acts 26). In 66 A.D. a riot broke out between the Jews and Syrians, helped by the Romans. The massacre of 20,000 Jews was the main cause of the great Jewish revolt which ended with the destruction of Jerusalem and the second Temple. In 69 A.D. Vespasian was proclaimed emperor here by his soldiers. In the 3rd century, the celebrated Christian scholar, Origen, founded a centre of Christian learning here. In 638, Caesarea passed into Moslem hands and in 1102 was occupied by the Crusaders. In 1252, King

The Crusader walls

Louis IX of France fortified the city by a wall and moat with an embankment. In 1291, Beybars devastated the city and completely destroyed it. This was the end of Caesarea, as the city was then abandoned and gradually buried under the sand dunes. It was only in 1956 that archaeologists began excavating Caesarea. Very important remains of the splendours of the city have been unearthed. From the Roman period were discovered the amphitheatre, which is in great part restored and used for concerts, the aqueduct which brought water to the city from the mountains 12 miles away, the hippodrome which is 1,000 feet long and accomodated 20,000 spectators and a stone inscribed with the name of Pontius Pilate which is the first archaeological evidence of the famous procurator who condemned Jesus to the cross.

Inscription of Pontius Pilate

The Roman Amphitheatre

The wall and gate at Caesarea are from the Crusader period. This wall, built by King Louis IX of France, was protected by a moat 30 feet wide and a sloping embankment 30—45 feet above the base of the moat. The Crusaders' city covered an area of 35 acres while the Roman city was about 6 times as large.

(Hill of Spring) was founded in 1909 on desolate sand dunes and is now the largest city in Israel with a population of 400,000. It is populated and administered entirely by Jews. It is the centre for commercial, industrial and cultural activities in Israel.

TEL AVIV

JAFFA

*...and went down
to Joppa, and he
found a ship...*
Jonah 1:3

is south of Tel-Aviv and has a population of 60,000. In contrast to Tel-Aviv, Jaffa has a recorded history of 3,600 years. It is mentioned in very early Egyptian and Assyrian documents — "And Jonah rose up to flee unto Tarshish from the presence of the Lord and went down to Jappo and he found a ship..." Jonah 1:3. Since very ancient times, it has been an important sea port for the country and the gateway to Jerusalem. The cedar wood of Lebanon for building Solomon's Temple and the rebuilding of the Temple under Zerubbabel, was unloaded here. At Jaffa, St. Peter raised Tabitha to life (Acts 9:36) and here St. Peter had the vision in which God asked him to preach also to the heathens the word of God. Today, Old Jaffa has become an "Art Centre" with bustling art galleries, jewellery shops and workshops.

Underwater scenery

RED SEA — EILAT

Since ancient times, the Red Sea was used as a major
route linking Asia and the Far East to Africa and the
West.

Being a continuation of the rift which extends from
mount Hermon in the North to the Gulf of Aqaba in
the south, the shores of the Red Sea reach great
depths which provide an ideal waterway for modern
shipping and an amazing colour of unbelievable blue.
Hidden in the depths as well as mingling among the
easily accessible coral reefs, live over 1000 unidenti-
fied species of sub-tropical fish, an untouched tre-
asure and paradise for deep sea divers and surface
snorklers.

And He gave unto Moses upon Mount Sinai, the two tablets of the testimony, tablets of stone, written with the finger of God.

Exodus 31:18

MOUNT SINAI

At the foot of Mount Sinai, the Monastery of Santa Caterina was erected, according to early Christian tradition, on the site of the Burning Bush. The holiness of this site attracted pilgrims and hermits from the earliest days of Christendom. It is named after St. Catherine of Alexandria who was martyred in the 4th century and whose bones, according to tradition, were transported to the peak of the nearby Mount Catherine. Served by devout Greek Orthodox monks, it houses the world's most unique and priceless collection of early icons as well as some 3000 ancient manuscripts that provide an unbroken history of more than 1500 years of Christianity.

EXODUS

Roaming Sinai and seeing the bedouins whose
mode of life in the desert has remained the same
for centuries is the easiest way to understand how
Moses led the children of Israel out of Egypt and
kept them wandering for 40 years in the wilderness
of Sinai.

D. Roberts, the Golden Gate (1839)

D. Roberts, the Citadel (1839)

D. Roberts, Church of the Holy Sepulchre

D. Roberts, Bethlehem (1839)

D. Roberts, Jerusalem (1839)

ONAGERS

...a joy of wild asses, a pasture of flocks.
Isaiah 32:14

IBEX

*...and went to seek David and his men
upon the rocks of the wild goats.* I Samuel 24:2

ADDAX

*...and the wild goat, and the Pygarg, and the wild ox, and
the chamois.* Deuteronomy 14:5

CORVUS

*...and to the young ravens
which cry...*
Psalms 147:9

CICONIA

*Yea, the stork in the heaven knoweth
her appointed times.*
Jeremiah 8:7

CAMEL

...with camels that bear spices...
I Kings 10:2

SCOLYMUS SP

Let thistles grow instead of wheat ... Job 31:40

LILLIUM CANDIUM

As the Lily among thorns ...

Song of Songs 2:2

CROCUS SP.

Spikenard and Saffron ...

Song of Songs

LINUM USITATISSIMUM

...and the flax and the barley...
Exodus 9:31

MANDRAGORA OFFICENARIUM

...and Reuben went in the days of wheat harvest and found mandrakes in the field... Genesis 30:14

RETAMA ROETAM
...and he lay and slept under a juniper tree...
Kings 19:5

NARCISSUS TAZETTA
*I am the rose of Sharon and
the lily of the valleys.*
Song of Songs 2:1

FLOWERS OF THE HOLY LAND

CENTAURA SP
*Thorns also and thistles
shall it bring forth to thee*
Genesis 3:18

PANCRATIUM SP
*As the Lily among thorns so is my love among
the daughters.*
Song of Songs 2:2

109

PEOPLE OF THE HOLY LAND

CAROB

And he would have fed on the pods that the swine ate. Luke 15:16

AMYGDALUS COMMUNIS

...and I said I see a road of an Almond tree. Jeremiah 1:11

PALMA

...the pomegranate tree, the palm tree also... Joel 1:12

ACACIA SP.

...and they shall make an ark of shittim wood...
Exodus 25:10

OLIVE

...and in her mouth was an olive leaf pluckt off...
Genesis 8:11